MYSTERIOUS MESSENGERS

Mysterious Messengers

*A Course on Hebrew Prophecy
from Amos Onwards*

John Eaton

WILLIAM B. EERDMANS PUBLISHING COMPANY
GRAND RAPIDS, MICHIGAN / CAMBRIDGE, U.K.

Originally published in 1997 by SCM Press Ltd
9-17 St Albans Place, London N1 0NX U.K.

This edition published in 1998 by
Wm. B. Eerdmans Publishing Co.
255 Jefferson Ave. S.E., Grand Rapids, Michigan 49503 /
P.O. Box 163, Cambridge CB3 9PU U.K.

Printed in the United States of America

02 01 00 99 98   5 4 3 2 1

ISBN 0-8028-4495-2 (pbk.: alk. paper)

For dearest Margaret

whose constant help has been of that biblical kind
better translated 'salvation'

In returning and rest you will be saved,
in stillness and trust shall be your strength

Contents

Preface

The ancient gurus were reputed to put many obstacles in the way of one who would be their disciple. They would be rude and repelling - all in order to test the applicant's mettle. When one approaches the Bible's prophetic books, one may no less be at first repelled. In these materials there is much that seems obscure, harsh, or lurid.

It was the achievement of nineteenth-century scholarship to penetrate the obscurity and show these prophets as great and ever-relevant figures. Indeed, enthusiasm for the prophets ran so high that they came to dominate our curricula and our entire understanding of the Old Testament. Eventually, short-comings in the rather restricted historical approach began to appear. The material often does not lend itself to precise questions of date and authorship. The increasingly complex academic debates began to seem fruitless and arid. The beginner might feel that the repelling gurus had come back again. So how to bring out again the attractive and wonderful qualities of the prophets, still taking account of what good scholarship over many years has established? To see the prophets with fresh wonder, it is necessary, I believe, to keep in mind their relation to the religious intermediaries of other peoples, to great poets of all times, and to their own liturgical tradition. In the present simple introduction, therefore, these relations are never far from our thoughts.

After four chapters on general matters, I introduce each prophetic book in turn, in roughly historical order, and end with Daniel to show the transition to apocalyptic literature. In the manner of a 'course', the chapters include boxes with numerous suggestions for simple research, for discussion, and for creative writing. Boxes are also used to give background information and comparative material. Full details of the books quoted there and in the text will be found in the bibliogtaphy. A final chapter offers summaries and broader thoughts on each prophet. I hope the course will prove useful in schools and higher education, as well as in the flourishing training ventures of the churches.

It was in fact to the Open Learning Centre that I owed the initial impulse, when I was asked to produce a course on the prophets. Writing those notes, and for several years assessing the resultant projects from all over the country, I saw the feasibility of a larger work. So I thank the Revd Roger Walton of the Centre for his encouragement, and for allowing me to take up something of that course into the present more ample treatment. I hope he will feel that his own aim of fostering enjoyable and imaginative study of theology has been carried through into this present book.

All at SCM Press I thank warmly, not least Margaret Lydamore for her expert guidance and editing. Gratefully too I recall the occasion of my first essay on the prophets for the Revd H. St J. Hart at Queens' College fifty-one years ago. He may notice some improvement since then, but I think he will like best my 'Voice of' pages, as he used to say that the best part of a sermon was the text.

John Eaton
June 1997

I

The Setting and Nature
of Hebrew Prophecy

A Near-Eastern view of life

Most people today plough their fields, go to war, cast their
vote, invest their money, have a family, see the doctor or go on
holiday – all in reliance on human knowledge. Our governments and councils make all their decisions through human
calculation.

But in the ancient Near East kings and peoples generally
believed that earth was under the rule of heaven. To govern,
direct a war, produce food, raise a family, go on a journey – in
all such things it was elementary prudence to learn, as far as
possible, what the heavenly power had in mind for you.

Near-Eastern link-persons

But how to get such knowledge? Throughout the Near East
there was a wide range of persons to whom you could turn, or
who themselves might feel impelled to visit you. These med-
iums or link-persons were known by various names signifying
kinds of priests, clairvoyants, astrologers and so on, and their
information came through a variety of means, such as trances,
or observation of omens in the stars or in animal entrails.
Where the means involved psychic gifts and resulted in impressive verbal pronouncements, we begin to see the figure of a
prophet.

Seers in Syria

From Mesopotamia and Syria we have records of quite a lot of prophetic visions and messages for kings. In an Aramaic inscription, King Zakir of Hamath (North Syria, 780 BCE) tells how he was besieged by Hazael king of Damascus (cf. I Kings 19. 15–17). He continues: 'I lifted up my hands to the Lord of heaven, who answered me and spoke to me through seers and messengers and said, Fear not, for I made you king and now will stand by you and deliver you.' (See further H. Ringgren, 'Prophecy in the Ancient Near East'.)

Intermediaries in Israel

The fundamentals in Israel were similar. God was seen as the king ruling all affairs of state and of individuals. It was as well to go with his purposes.

Terms for the various kinds of people who would make a link for you with God's mysterious work covered priests, levites, diviners, seers and other devotees. Among these, we especially connect with prophecy those termed *hozeh* ('visionary'), *ro'eh* ('seer'), *ish (ha-)elohim* ('man of God', 'holy man'), *nabi* ('spokesman', 'prophet') and *nbi'a* ('prophetess'). These terms for prophetic types became rather interchangeable, and in the end it was *nabi* which became the umbrella term.

Becoming a prophet

How did people become recognized prophets in Israel? It is likely that on the one hand there was personal spiritual experience, a 'call', and on the other hand support and training from an established group. Such a situation in modern West Africa is described by E.G.Parrinder (*African Traditional Religion*, ch.IX). He relates how an individual may first have a trance-like experience, then be attached to a holy centre for a time, perhaps returning to the centre for periods in later life, and always remaining liable to supranormal states.

While there is no general information on the question in the Old Testament, it is interesting that accounts of particular experiences of vocation often show an institutional connection. We have several vivid glimpses of persons already in the sphere of sanctuary or priesthood suddenly being made messengers of great events (I Sam. 3; Isa. 6; Jer.1; Ezek.1–3).

A *two-way service*

It seemed obvious that, as king over all, God would want to issue orders and decisions. From his initiative then, prophets, as his 'servants', were commissioned, informed, and sent to bear his orders and decisions to the people concerned. Hence, they often spoke in the style of ordinary message-bearers: 'Thus says the Lord to so-and-so, Behold, I . . .'

For your research

Looking at the 'call' stories in I Sam. 3, Isa. 6, Jer. 1 and Ezek. 1–3, can you say:

– Where exactly were Samuel and Isaiah when they were called?

– What exactly was Jeremiah appointed to be?

– Which prophet is said to have had experience of the Spirit at his call?

But this role as messengers of God was only half their duty. People came to them to act for them towards God, to approach God on their behalf. They asked the prophet to ascertain God's will for them. And even more, they asked him or her to pray for their relief or healing. 'He is a nabi,' one text says, 'and if *he* prays for you, you will recover' (Gen. 20.7).

Gaining heavenly knowledge

The prophets needed a way of obtaining the knowledge requested in such specific consultations. Various references show how they might keep a long vigil of meditation (Jer. 42.7; Hab. 2.1; Isa. 50.4) and how the playing of a harp might help bring the moment of illumination (II Kings 3.15). The music and dancing of the prophetic groups might also lead to that heightened consciousness where heavenly knowledge came (I Sam. 10.5–6, 10; I Kings 22.11–12).

Things actually seen, or perceived only by the inner eye, could also become windows of revelation. Examples include a blossoming bough (Jer. 1.11–12), a steaming pot (Jer. 1.13–14), a swarm of locusts and a basket of summer fruit (Amos 7.1–3; 8.1–3).

Potent words and acts

Prophets were thought to act for God not only by speaking words, but also by doing dramatic actions in imitation of the foreshadowed event. The words themselves were considered power-filled, dealing hammer-blows (Jer. 23.29), effective as the rains (Isa.55.10–11). But the dramatic actions also were considered to be potent expressions of God's will, launching his work. When Elisha laid his hands on the king's hands and the king shot the arrow through the window, it was the Lord's arrow, initiating victory (II Kings 13.15–17).

Though this practice seems somewhat akin to magic, a distinction can be made. Imitative magic is designed to effect a human purpose. The prophetic action, however, was seen as expressing the purpose of God and enacted only as a result of his compulsion on the prophet. It was often very unwelcome to the beholders (e.g. Jer. 19.1–2, 10–11).

The age and distinctiveness of Hebrew prophecy

When we consider prophecy in its fundamentals, we can allow that the Hebrew people had always had some form of it. But when we focus on a particular kind of Hebrew prophecy, we see it flourishing only in some specific period of the people's history. The fundamental ideas and practices grew naturally, like the Hebrew language itself, from Israel's roots in the ancient Near East. But special forms, such as the massed ec-statics, the heroic individuals, and eventually the production of a great prophetic literature, arose in particular periods. Each form was connected with its own special circumstances and was not really repeated.

It is valuable to begin, as we have done, by seeing the roots, ways, and many of the practitioners of Hebrew prophecy as part of a shared Near-Eastern culture. But as we are carried by our studies ever deeper into the prophetic writings of the Bible, we shall become aware of something unique and extremely impressive. We may trace this greatness in four respects:

1. *Criticism of society.* Some prophets address the whole nation, or many nations, with radical condemnation of abuse of power.

2. *Visions of salvation.* Linked to the condemnation came prophecy of a new world and an ideal ruler. And so a great two-sided vision of the ultimate future developed – doom and new creation – which was to have enormous influence.

3. *Personal dedication.* Hebrew prophecy offers some rich examples of a life given over to God, and so impinging all the more on society. Such a prophet was thought to become a 'sign', an incarnation of a message from God.

4. *The prophetic literature.* From care to preserve words spoken when the nation faced doom, words that gave meaning and hope in the darkest days, grew the prophetic books. This literature, a vast tapestry of world doom and re-birth, is certainly unique.

For discussion or writing

– In the story of Ex. 4.10–16, Aaron is to be 'mouth' for Moses, and Moses 'god' for Aaron. In Ex. 7.1–2 Moses acts as 'god' and Aaron as 'nabi'. Looking carefully at these passages, can you use them to clarify the work of a nabi?

– It was recently said of modern Italy that more people go to the magician than to Mass. Are there in fact more parallels in modern life to the ancient Near-Eastern use of link-persons than we might have supposed?

– Even before entering our present study of the Hebrew prophets, we are sure to have experienced something of their contribution to religious and moral thought. Suggest some examples now, and return to the subject when our present studies are concluded.

Pegs in the wall of history

---

c. 1300 BCE (?)	Moses
c. 1230–1030	The Judges
1010–970	David reigns. He captures ancient city of Jerusalem *c.* 1000.
970–931	Solomon reigns. He extends Jerusalem to northern hill with temple and palace.
931	Northern Israel (with most of the tribes) splits off as separate kingdom.
745–727	Tiglath Pileser III king of Assyria (northern Iraq).
733	Assyria annexes Gilead and Galilee from N. Israel.
721	Assyria annexes Samaria and rest of N. Israel. Deportations.

711	Assyria crushes resistance centred at (Philistine) Ashdod.
701	Assyria under Sennacherib crushes resistance in Judah. 46 towns destroyed. 200,150 people deported. Jerusalem under Hezekiah submits and survives.
from 627	Assyria declines after the death of King Ashur-bani-pal. Judah expands under King Josiah.
621	Josiah's religious reforms. He abolishes sanctuaries outside Jerusalem.
from 605	Babylon under Nebuchadnezzar becomes new world power.
597	Babylonians quell revolt and capture Jerusalem. King Jehoiachin is deported with many citizens, including Ezekiel. Zedekiah is installed as king.
586/7	Babylonians quell second revolt, destroy Jerusalem and temple, deport Zedekiah and many citizens, and install Judean governor (Gedaliah) at Mizpah, 8 miles north of Jerusalem.
from 586/2	Gedaliah murdered. Remaining Judean leaders flee to Egypt, taking Jeremiah.
539	Cyrus the Persian overcomes the Babylonians and soon allows Jewish exiles to return and temple to be refounded.
515	New temple completed in Jerusalem.
333	Persian empire gives way to the Greek.
167–164	Antiochus IV (Greek ruler based in Syria) persecutes traditionalist Judaism.
from 164	Judah gains independence under the priestly family of Hashmon (the 'Maccabees').
from 63	Palestine in sphere of Rome.
70 CE	Rome crushes revolt and destroys Jerusalem.

2

Great Crises – Great Prophets

Great spirits answering catastrophe

In the eighth century BCE the twin Hebrew kingdoms (Northern Israel and Judah, with their capitals Samaria and Jerusalem) passed from prosperity to catastrophe. Towards the end of the century, the military machine of the vast Assyrian empire crushed the kingdom of Samaria and terribly reduced that of Jerusalem. But from the ruins were preserved words of four radical prophets – Amos, Hosea, Isaiah and Micah. Nothing quite like them is known from earlier times. The depth of the crisis seems to have evoked an extraordinary depth of ministry. Their work will have been preserved precisely because it showed meaning in all the darkness of destruction and deportation.

Though the Jerusalem kingdom just survived, its final downfall came early in the sixth century. The Babylonian empire had by now succeeded the Assyrian, and it was to settlements in Babylonia that the survivors of Jerusalem's leading classes were marched away for an exile of half a century or more.

Jeremiah was active in the last decades of royal Jerusalem and beyond. Ezekiel preached to the exiles. Successors of Isaiah (Isa. 40–66) bridged the period when the Persian empire replaced the Babylonian and restored the community (but not the monarchy) in and around Jerusalem.

The end of a prophetic era

Other prophetic ministries left deposits – smaller but notable – in the collection of prophetic books, including Zephaniah, Nahum and Habakkuk from the seventh century and Haggai, Zechariah and Malachi from the sixth to the fifth. But the great series of voices died out with changing conditions. The end of the independent royal state, the rise of a ruling priesthood, the construction of a massive scripture, the framework of Persian and then Greek empire – all may have contributed to the end of the great prophetic sequence.

But now in the form of books the radical words lived on. In this abiding form they still had power to quicken religious impulses and movements.

Taking old truth seriously

In assessing the greatness of such as Amos, Isaiah or Jeremiah, modern scholars used to portray them as original thinkers, milestones in the upward progress of religious sensitivity and understanding. Such prophets were seen as individual geniuses, rising above the mass religion to declare for the first time the oneness of God, his righteousness, and his demand for justice and compassion rather than sacrifice.

It has gradually become apparent, however, that in all this the prophets were drawing on older teaching. Theirs was rather the merit of seeing and speaking out clearly in a time of corruption and confusion. They were brave, radical and timely spokesmen of the truth. Above all, they saw and lived for the *application* of the ancient truth, its bearing on the society and politics of their day.

Bring no more vain offerings!

The great prophets sometimes spoke scathingly about particular places of worship and the manner of worship, especially the offering of sacrifice. Throughout the Near East, the ideas connected with sacrifice could sometimes be crude – as though the gods depended on it for food. Even short of this crudity, worshippers in Israel could easily slip into feeling that through sacrifices they were putting God into their debt. Here was a fundamental error which the discerning prophets, jealous of God's sovereignty, included in their denunciations. But, as we shall see, they were not necessarily proposing a worship completely without offerings.

---

incense, drink (prayer)

commitment no

sin → pure

For your research

Along with sacrifice, what other forms of worship are rejected in Isa.1.10–20? What reason is given? Could the rejection, according to this passage, be withdrawn?

Solitaries and laymen?

Their condemnation of shrines, worship and sacred officials makes the great prophets appear as individual outsiders, laymen and unofficial, set over against the religious institutions and the professional holy men and women. But severe critics can arise from within the institution, all the more mordant because of their inside knowledge. The priestly origins of Jeremiah and Ezekiel happen to be mentioned in their books, and if most of the great prophets had some association with the holy centres and personnel, it would be easier to understand their command of sacred language and tradition, their opportunities to teach at festivals, and the preservation of their teachings after their death – not by isolated sects, but by official channels, in the end to become national scripture.

An unnecessary confusion is caused by some modern translations of Amos 7.14 as 'I am not a prophet . . .' Anticipating our study of Amos, we may think the older translations wiser with 'I was not a prophet nor a son of a prophet, but I was a herdsman . . .' Amos is then referring to his call to become a prophet and change his way of life as evidence that the Lord now really speaks through him. (We might compare Paul's argument in Gal. 1.11–14.)

Not just a shepherd?

In Amos 1.1, Amos is described as having been among the *noqdim* of Tekoa (a few miles south of Bethlehem). The only other occurrence of this term in the Bible refers to the king of Moab (who would be a sacred figure) as keeping large flocks (II Kings 3.4). Abroad, the term occurs on the North Syrian coast, where a man was chief of these persons and also chief of the priests. In Mesopotamia the term denoted keepers of large flocks which might be linked with temples. On this basis, the prominent Swedish scholar Ivan Engnell concluded that *noqdim* in Amos 1.1 probably referred to a group of temple herdsmen, servants of the Jerusalem temple, who managed its herds and properties in the district of Tekoa (see Engnell's *Critical Essays on the Old Testament,* p.133).

The mouth and the pen

'Hear this' is a typical beginning to a prophet's saying, and indeed the evidence generally indicates that a prophet would, face to face, speak or chant his message, which had come to him already in artistic form in a time of intense concentration. The prophets were not writers, adjusting and trimming their words. The story of Jer. 36 shows how sayings carried in the memory for over twenty years might in special circumstances be dictated by the prophet to an assistant skilled in writing. In fact this particular writing soon perished, solemnly cut up and burned by the king, but thanks to the prophet's memory the words were still not lost, but could be dictated again. This was a special case, but it is an example of the fact that in one way or another, for one purpose of another, traditions of sayings of the great prophets came to be put into writing.

Editing and sub-editing

Processes of arranging and augmenting the sayings took place before the books reached their present form. Traces of those who handled the traditions and documents appear in various ways. Note how they refer to the prophet in the third person in Amos 1.1–2; 7.12–14; similarly Hosea 1.1–6 and often in other prophetic books.

In the Book of Isaiah there are various editorial headings and signs of development over several centuries. In the Book of Jeremiah, his sensitive poetry is embedded in much prose of heavy style and in extensive biography. In the Book of Ezekiel there are duplications and signs of much annotation by editors with priestly concerns.

Circles and disciples

The story of the completion of the prophetic books is not recorded. We can only look for clues in the character of the material. There is no account to tell us clearly who were these circles posited by modern scholars under such names as 'the Deuteronomists', 'Levites', 'the Isaiah school'.

There are a few references to disciples or assistants of the great prophets (Isa. 8.16–22; 50.4; Jer. 36; cf. I Sam. 19.20; I Kings 19.19–21; II Kings 2). This slender evidence becomes significant when account is taken of the role of disciples generally in the ancient Near East. It is well known, for example, that Arabian

---

A glimpse of the meditating disciples

In my book *Festal Drama in Deutero-Isaiah* (p.70) I gave the following interpretation of Isaiah 50.4, a verse where the word *limmudim*, 'disciples', occurs twice:

The limmudim *here, as in Isaiah 8.16, are young prophets, apprentices in the master's circle whom he sends out to extend his ministry. Their 'tongue' is one which bears a faith-strengthening oracle of God. As for the 'mornings', the point would be that the prophetic circle together practise long vigils of concentration on God's will, rather like the corporate meditation of Buddhist monks. At dawn especially, God stirs up his oracular word in the ear of one of them.*

poets and Jewish rabbis relied on a system of committing their compositions or teachings to disciples for a solemn handing down through generations. This was the appropriate way of extending and prolonging their work. It seems likely that a similar service of disciples formed a bridge between the first preaching of the great prophets and the emergence of their books.

For discussion or writing

Having in mind remarks about the prophets in this chapter, can you

– compare some modern examples of 'a critic from within the institution'

– give examples of people of recent centuries who were noted for originality, but all the same built on achievements of their predecessors?

3

The Poetry and Patterns
of Prophecy

Prophets like bards

Life on a large housing estate can seem tedious at times, and it seemed especially so in the heat by the waterways outside Babylon around 580 BCE. There the exiled citizens of Jerusalem would sit in the shade of their walls and doorways, glad to pass round any news. Sometimes an exciting report spread that there was to be a gathering to hear a message from their prophet-priest. They anticipated it with relish, just as if they were going to hear a skilled singer of love-songs accompanied by the heavenly notes of his lyre. This comparison (given in Ezek. 33.30–33) may have come to mind because prophets gave their utterances in poetic form, and hence in chanted style, and were known to use musical instruments (I Chron. 25).

Publication by chant

In her remarkable book *Poetry and Prophecy* (p.1), N. Kershaw Chadwick writes:

In the greater part of the ancient world, poetry was not a thing to be read, but to be heard, and to be heard by as many people as possible. This was the only form of publication. And so oral poetry was not generally recited, but rather sung or chanted.

Rhythm

A glance at a modern English Bible reveals that a large part of the prophetic books has poetic form, which is printed in short lines, often with every second line indented. The rhythm of the lines in the Hebrew original is not as strict and unvaried as in traditional European poetry, but all the same a rhythmic beat is there. If we count the major stresses in a line, we often find two balancing parts giving a beat of 3+3. We can imitate this in translation, the indented English line representing the second part of the Hebrew line. Thus Isa. 40.6:

> The voice of one saying, cry!
> And one says, What shall I cry?
> All mortals are no better than grass,
> their faithfulness fades like a flower.

Changing the rhythm for effect

There are other favourite rhythms. Urgently Isa. 1.2 begins with 2+2+2:

> Hear O heavens,
> hearken earth,
> for the Lord has spoken.

A special intensity comes with shortening of the last part of the Hebrew line. Thus Amos 5.19:

> as if someone fled from the face of a lion
> and was met by a bear,
> then escaped to his house and leaned on the wall
> and a snake bit him.

Such rhythms are varied with freedom as the prophet's inspiration flows – spontaneous, though assisted by traditional styles.

Spell-bound

In her *Poetry and Prophecy* (p.47) N.K.Chadwick describes the awe with which the chanted recitation is heard:

When a (Siberian) shaman is reciting, not a sound escapes from the audience, their pipes go out, their eyes are riveted on the shaman, and for a long time after he has ceased to speak no one moves. All are spell-bound.

Patterns of thought and expression

A major feature of this poetry is 'parallelism'. Many of the thoughts are expressed twice over, or at least there is a balance between the two (occasionally three) parts of a line. If not repeating the thought exactly, the second part may gather it up and complete it, or extend it, or reinforce it in a contrasting style, or at the least match it in rhythm.

Thus patterns of tersely expressed thought are built up, achieving appropriate effects – emphasis, fear, jubilation, suspense and resolution.

In addition to these patterns of 'parallelism', the prophets used most of the patterns (or 'forms') of public eloquence that had developed through many centuries. For each kind of social and religious situation a style had developed. Thus there was a particular shape or style of utterance for supplicatory prayer, for God's responding messages of salvation, for his warnings and threats, for hymns, for launching sacred processions, for funeral dirges, for proverbs, for wedding songs, for judicial speeches, for taunting foes, for ridiculing rival gods, for God's designation of a new king, for cries of the water-seller, and so on. Such traditional patterns of speech were used by the prophets – not pedantically, but as spring-boards for their flights of eloquence. Isa. 40–55 has been analysed by some scholars into about seventy units of speech, which can each be labelled as one or other of such traditional 'forms'; yet the style is anything but stilted and stale, being on the contrary remarkably brilliant.

For your consideration

Think of examples in speech today where styles and shapes have developed for particular uses or occasions. Are there favourite phrases or themes which characterize advertisements, sermons, spontaneous prayers, television presenters?

Sound-play

Such poetry may be said to rhyme thoughts rather than sounds. But while there is little use of rhymes in the manner beloved by most of our poetry, there is still some play on the sounds of the Hebrew words. The translator fortunately can reproduce the pattern of thoughts, but can rarely do justice to the sound-effects achieved in the Hebrew. Where the English has 'If you do not believe, surely you will not be established' (Isa. 7.9), the Hebrew has:

> *im lo ta'aminu*
> *ki lo te'amenu.*

Where English has 'Gilgal shall surely go into exile' (Amos 5.5), Hebrew has:

> *haggilgal galo yigleh.*

Imagery

It came easily to Hebrew poet-prophets to fill their utterance with powerful imagery from Nature. The natural world was for them no soulless environment, but a living part of God's universal community. When the Lord utters his lion-roar from his royal throne, green hills grow pale and the lush summits of Mount Carmel wither (Amos 1.2). As Jeremiah (4.10–26) grieves over his people's skill in evil and ignorance of right, he sees the skies dark, the mountains moving, people vanished, birds all fled, fruitful land become desert, cities in ruins. When a great successor of Isaiah (55.12) announces the reign of God in salvation, he sees the mountains break forth into singing and the trees of the forest dance and clap their hands.

From both town and country the prophets drew powerful imagery for comparisons – justice like an ever-flowing stream (Amos 5.24), complacent religious leaders like over-fed guard-dogs (Isa. 56.10), an inspired prophet staggering like a drunken man (Jer. 23.9), people who go after other gods like a she-camel or a wild ass on heat (Jer. 2.23–24), commitment that evaporates like the morning dew (Hos. 6.4).

Pictures and comparisons, metaphors and similes, shifting colours and rhythms – all abound in the poetry of the prophets, a language of heightened imagination and swiftly-flowing inspiration.

Poetry and God

When the prophet makes solemn intercession to God, he still speaks in poetry, using especially the traditional style of the lamenting psalms (e.g. Hab. 1.2–4). If he hears a response from God, it will also be in poetry (e.g. Hab. 1.5–11).

This illustrates how poetry is fitting for communications of

Poetry, prophecy and song

N.K. Chadwick (*Poetry and Prophecy*, p.45) helps us again:

Wherever poetry is a highly cultivated art, prophetic utterance is couched in poetical form and (may be) accompanied by music in some form. The Greek word . . . for the oracular voice of a deity is (ultimately) identical with our word 'song'.

deep intensity. It shows too that the thoughts passing between God and the prophet and from prophet to people have come to expression in moments of concentrated attention, when minds are focussed to the essential.

Divine power in poetry

The idea of poetry as holy and potent can be illustrated by some brilliant passages depicting the downfall of an evil power (Assyria in Nahum 2.1–3.4, Babylon in Isa. 46.1–2, Jer. 51). Although sometimes sounding like eye-witness descriptions from the midst of the battles, they are actually prophecies given in advance and far away, intended as symbolic blows of God against his foes.

The anticipatory nature of these portrayals of conflict is shown by the fact that events actually turned out rather differently. The city of Babylon, for example, was entered by the Persian conquerors without a battle, Cyrus being hailed as a saviour restoring proper order.

For discussion or writing

– How important is poetry in worship today? How does the use of music relate to such poetry? Is there a connection with dance?

– Here are five half-lines of a prophet's poem, each of which is now lacking its parallel statement. Can you compose suitable half-lines to fill the gaps – and then see how Jeremiah did it (4.23–26)?

a) I beheld the earth and lo, it was waste and void . . .

b) I beheld the mountains and lo, they trembled . . .

c) I beheld and lo, there was no man . . .

d) I beheld and lo, the fruitful field was a wilderness . . .

e) at the presence of the Lord . . .

4

Favourite Themes and Words

One true God

A gradual progress towards monotheism, completed about 550 BCE in the great teachings of Isaiah 40–55 – such was the way scholars used to present the view of God in the prophets. They believed that it was largely from these pioneering prophets that the conception of the one sole God passed into other streams of biblical thought.

But with increasing knowledge of the ancient world, the picture has changed. Many psalms which praise God as universal Creator (such as 24, 29, 93, 104) can now be seen as much older than the prophets. Amos, Isaiah and others will have inherited a conception of 'the Lord' (Hebrew 'Yahweh') as sovereign over all, the true and incomparable God, though surrounded, worshipped and served by many divine beings. The great prophets indeed generally assume and start from the uniqueness of Yahweh, the Most High, the King of kings.

Not that polytheism was dead. In other nations it flourished alongside quite ancient glimpses of monotheism. In Israel it had a tendency to revive, down to quite late periods, although sometimes fiercely opposed and condemned. It is not surprising, therefore, that the relatively late prophet in Isaiah 40–55 should spell out the nature of Yahweh as the unique eternal God. The teaching needed re-asserting, especially because of the circumstances of the exile in Babylonia.

Holiness and glory

Sometimes the prophets dwell on God's 'holiness' (*qodesh*). Just as Ps. 99 is built on three-fold praise of Yahweh's holiness (vv. 3, 5, 9) as he shows his kingly power to the worshippers at Zion, so Isaiah saw and heard divine beings thrice acclaiming that same holiness of the universal king revealed in the temple (Isa. 6.3). This prophet especially entitled God 'the Holy One of Israel' (31.1 etc). Ezekiel often spoke of God purposing to show forth his

---

Harmonizing the faiths

In the ancient Near East there was sometimes a tendency to harmonize the worship of the One and the many. From Egypt we have hymns which treat the traditional gods as aspects of the one Creator; here is an example from about 1300 BCE:

I sing to you intoxicated by your beauty.
My hands upon the minstrel's harp,
I teach the company of the singers
how to worship the beauty of your face.

Praise to you . . . who spoke with your mouth
and there came into being all people and gods,
all animals, large and small,
and all creatures of the air.

Do not widows say 'You are my husband'
and little ones 'Our father and mother'?
The rich praise your beauty
and the poor worship your face.
To you the prisoner turns.
Those who are sick cry out to you.

Green plants turn towards him
so that they may be beautiful,
and lotuses are happy because of him.

(For a full translation see Pritchard (ed), *Ancient Near Eastern Texts*, p.371b.)

holiness, to disclose with full power the holiness of his name (36.23–32), a tremendous, world-transforming event.

In such passages, 'holiness' is the essence of God's being, his awesome otherness. If places, times, or people are sometimes also called 'holy', the meaning is that in a special way they are touched or possessed by God, made special instruments of his working.

Another term for the expression of God's holy being was 'glory' (*kabod*), an incomparable weight of excellence, a unique majesty (Ps. 29.9; Isa. 6.3). Although the Hebrew term has a basic sense of 'heaviness' rather than 'brightness', the weight and worth of God's person are felt, as it were, to create a tremendous aura, more than enough to fill the whole earth. Hence there are passages where this 'glory' is seen as a wonderful radiance by the prophetic eye (Isa. 60.1).

Yahweh – judge of all nations

The psalms had long recognized Yahweh's power to judge all nations (Ps.2; 9.5–8; 11.4 etc). The prophets followed this tradition in seeing him as able to direct and judge all the earth's population. Sometimes they listed guilty nations in an order representing the four points of the compass, so symbolizing Yahweh's judgment of the whole world from his throne. The temple at 'Zion' (in effect Jerusalem seen as a sacred place) was itself a symbol of the heavenly throne, and so at the centre of earthly life (we shall note such thought in Amos 1–2 and Zeph. 2–3 etc).

'Judging' and 'judgment' in Hebrew are usually more concerned with the continual work of ruling and governing than our English words suggest. The ideal of Yahweh's ruling all nations was never far from the thoughts of the great prophets. For all nations, as for Israel, his rule or 'judgment' was righteous, upholding an order of right and goodness, saving the oppressed (Ps. 9.4–12; 96.10–13; Isa. 5.16–17).

God of Israel/Jacob

This universal God and Creator was nevertheless said to be in special relation to the people of Israel, to the dynasty of David, and to Zion. No contradiction was seen here. So the old psalms sang of God Most High (supreme over all) having his abode in Zion (Ps. 48 etc). There he channelled his reign through the dynasty of David (Ps. 72). Israel as a people was specially owned by him, blessed since the Exodus with his special presence (Ps. 114).

With such traditional beliefs the prophets worked in one way or another. The actual word 'covenant' (*brith*) to express the Lord's relationship with Israel and David scarcely appears in the prophets earlier than Jeremiah. But the basic idea of such a bond is everywhere apparent. The Lord speaks of Israel as 'my people', a family he has reared from birth (Isa. 1.2–3). Of all the nations, them only has he known – this idiom in Amos 3.2 (as is now evident from its use in Near Eastern treaties and inscriptions) means that he has selected them and watched over them, so that they should serve him in a leading task. We may compare the picturesque conception of Ex. 19.5–6, where the Lord of all the world will have the whole nation as a priesthood mediating his grace to all nations – but with an 'If'!

The mysterious name

The very common name of God in the Hebrew scriptures is 'Yahweh'. It seems to have been used in the Sinai region long before the time of Moses. It was only in quite late times that its use in speech was avoided out of reverence. In Hebrew, then in Greek (and so eventually in English Bibles) one now said 'the Lord' instead of 'Yahweh'. (In some passages, however, the original name is important for the sense. In such cases translators in the Reformation put 'Jehovah', a confused version of 'Yahweh'.)

The meaning of the name has been much debated, But it may well have meant 'HE IS/HE WHO IS', an expression of unique and mysterious reality and consequent authority. The account in Ex. 3.13–15 is then, after all, our best guide.

The nature of sin

The wrongdoing of Israel seemed all the more hurtful because of the bond and the high calling. Their sins were an abuse of God's love, a forgetting of all God's care, a rebellion against a good father (Isa. 1.2), a betrayal (Hos. 6.7), infidelity as of a wayward spouse (Hos. 1.2; 2.2; Ezek. 16.15). Sin, in short, was a breach in the relationship with the Lord.

For consideration

In the light of what has been said in this chapter about 'holiness', which of these translations of Ezek. 36.23 do you prefer, and can you do better?

I will sanctify my great name.

I will hallow my great name.

I will vindicate the holiness of my great name.

I will display the holiness of my great name.

The form of Israel's sin

For the prophets, Israel's offence against her Lord took two main forms. First there was oppression of the poor. In a country where people subsisted on the current year's growth, and where the rains sometimes failed, many would quickly fall into debt and bondage. Powerful people were exploiting this situation ruthlessly and callously. The great prophets brought words of searing condemnation from the Lord (Amos 2.6–7; 4.1; Isa. 5.7; Micah 2.1–2; 3.1–3).

The other main form which the sinfulness took was the worship of 'other gods'. The worship of Yahweh as sole Lord was weakened and blurred by recourse to ideas and rituals resurfacing from the older religions of the country and, later, imported from the empires of Assyria and Babylon. Along with the worship of named gods and goddesses, there might be shifts in the understanding of Yahweh himself, all in the direction of the worship of fertility, leading to sexual excesses, magical practices, and even child sacrifice. This trend was condemned by prophets as 'adultery' or 'prostitution' committed by Yahweh's 'wife' Israel (Hos. 1.2; 2.5; Jer. 2.9–13; Ezek. 16.15).

From a dictionary entry on 'sin'

The famous Hastings' *Dictionary of the Bible* has the following remarks on 'sin' (p.918):

It was the prophetic function to deepen the consciousness of sin by revealing a God of moral righteousness to a people whose peculiar relationship to Yahweh involved both immense privileges and grave responsibilities . . . The first two verses of Psalm 51 are instructive in ideas of sin . . . Here there are three words used for 'sin' . . . The first is the Hebrew *pesha'*, which strictly means 'rebellion' . . . so that sin is not the transgression of a code of morals so much as a personal rebellion against God . . . The second word is *'awon*, which describes sin as a deliberate turning aside out of the way . . . The third word is *ḥaṭṭath*, which describes sin as missing the mark . . . not wilfully but because of the weakness of human kind.

Repentance as homecoming

Prophetic calls to repentance were therefore expressed not so much as exhortations to get back to a moral code, but as appeals to come back to a personal relationship with the Lord. The people should 'return' to their God (Isa. 10. 21; 55.7; Hos. 6.1; Ezek. 18.30), 'seek' the Lord (Amos 5.4–6), 'know' the Lord again (Hos. 6.3; Jer. 31.34).

How vividly Zephaniah portrayed the shocking state of the 'holy' city! The rulers preyed on the weak like hunting lions or ravening wolves, prophets were deceivers, priests profaned the temple (3.1–5). But vivid too was his vision of the city as she would be redeemed: the Lord comes to his bride Zion, dances and sings songs of love to her – the restoration indeed of a personal bond, though characteristically one which embraces the community (3.14–18)!

Some of the prophets' own words

---

qadosh	holy	*mishpaṭ*	justice
kabod	glory	*ḥesed*	enduring love
ṣedeq	right(eousness)	*shub*	to return

The following words are formed from the same root – can you see any logical connection between them?

amen	surely	*eme(n)t*	truth
emunah	faithfulness	*he'emin*	to trust

Grace and compassion

Our reference to Zephaniah's vision of restoration also illustrates how hope came to rest chiefly on the grace of God. The great prophets came to see the chances of repentance as slender indeed. Divine punishment which would devastate the national structures appeared inevitable (Amos 8.1–2). Where hope did emerge, it was founded on conviction of God's perseverance with his original good purpose, on his enduring grace and compassion, rather than on human possibilities. Because of the divine commitment in *ḥesed*, the love that was 'for ever' (Ps. 136), hope could blossom.

The visions of hope take various forms, all the more precious because seen by those who have also recognized evil with terrible clarity. A new shoot would spring from the royal stump (Isa. 11.1). A humble remnant of the people would be built up again (Zeph. 2.3, 7; 3.12, 13). God would give a new spirit and a new and sensitive heart to the people (Ezek. 36.24–27). From death-like exile, they would be restored to fullness of life before God's face, as it were by a blast of the divine Spirit-wind upon the bones of the long dead (Ezek. 37.1–14).

The great pilgrimage-festival

Although some passages tell us of three main occasions in the year when the people were to gather at Yahweh's sanctuary, the evidence indicates that one of these observances was pre-eminent in the period from about 1200–400 BCE. It fell around the time of the autumnal new year, when the annual agricultural cycle was shortly to begin, and when it therefore seemed especially urgent to renew the relationship with the Lord, and earnestly pray for the rains and other blessings needed for growth.

It is sometimes simply called 'the (pilgrimage) festival' (the *ḥag*) or 'the festival of Yahweh', and at other times people spoke of Ingathering (Asiph) or Booths/Tabernacles (Sukkoth). The precise details of its date and duration in this period are not known, but in some way it formed the antecedents of the holy season fixed in later times with a New Year's Day, Day of Atonement, and week of Booths (days 1, 10, and 15–22 of the month of Tishri, September–October). For ancient peoples especially, such a festival of renewal was immensely important. They felt that they found new life from God; his fountain sprang anew for them; his light of life shone upon them.

While discovery of the importance of this festival seemed to bring a new dimension to modern understanding of the Bible, some scholars took a negative attitude towards it, stressing the limitations in the explicit evidence. But a great deal in the psalms and prophets will be missed if this festival is not borne in mind. Speeches of God to his assembled people, such as we often find in the prophets, found their opportunity here, when the Lord was believed to come into the midst of the great gathering of pilgrims. Many themes in the speeches connect with the concerns of the festival. Sin atonement, the processional advent of God, the new manifestation of his kingship, the role of his 'Servant' from the house of David, the prospects for peace and plenty in the new year

– such topics of prophecy will be better understood when (often by reference to the Psalms) their roots in the great festival are recognized.

For discussion or writing

– Find some examples in the Bible where the word 'holy' is applied to people or things on earth, and suggest in each case why this term has been used.

– The prophets often speak of the nation as though it were a great person, a 'corporate personality'. From references given in this chapter, note some examples, and consider the gain and loss in this way of thinking. Does the subject have any bearing on the concern with corporate identity in modern management?

THE VOICE OF AMOS

This is what the the Lord says:
  For sin upon sin of Israel
    I will not call back the doom,
  for they sell the innocent for silver
    and the poor for a pair of sandals (2.6-7).

Hear this word, family of Israel,
  which the Lord has spoken for you.
You were my choice from all the families of the earth
and therefore I shall deal with you for all your wrongdoing
                                                    (3.1-2).

If you would live, seek the Lord,
  lest he break out like fire,
you who change justice into poison
  and knock righteousness to the ground.
The maker of Orion and the Pleiad stars,
  who can change morning to the shadow of death
    and darken day into night,
who called up the waters of the sea
  and poured them on the face of the earth,
his name is the Lord —
  he can make ruin blaze upon the mighty (5.6-8).

Relieve me of the noise of your hymns!
  I would not hear the music of your harps!
But let justice roll like waters
        and righteousness like an ever-flowing stream! (5.23-24).

Are you not the same as the Ethiopians to me,
  O people of Israel, says the Lord?
Israelites from Egypt,
  Philistines from Caphtor, Syrians from Kir,
  did I not bring up them all? (9.7).

5

Amos – The Lion's Roar

Here we meet the earliest of the ministries giving rise to a prophetic book. As the Book of Amos is also outstandingly clear, compact and forceful, it will be worthwhile for us now to follow it through in some detail.

A note from the editors

The arrangers of the material have headed it with some brief information (Amos 1.1). They offer us 'the words of Amos', his poetic speeches. The name 'Amos' seems to be short for 'Amasiah' (II Chron. 17.16), 'The Lord has carried' or 'Carried by the Lord' – he has taken up the child in his arms.

We are told that Amos had been among the sheep-farmers of Tekoa. This fortified town was a few miles south-east of Bethlehem, where you might find fertile pockets in the stony hill-sides, close to the grim desert that crumples its way down steeply to the Dead Sea.

The date of the revelations is noted: when Uzziah reigned in Judah (783–742) and Jeroboam II in Israel (Samaria, 786–746), and more precisely, 'two years before the earthquake'. This suggests that Amos had warned of doom in a concentrated period of prophesying, and that confirmation or partial fulfilment was seen shortly afterwards in the occurrence of an earthquake. There is evidence of a considerable earthquake between 760 and 750 BCE, and this is the likely date of the main explosion of the mission of Amos.

It was a time when the great military power of Assyria

(Northern Iraq) had subdued Israel's traditional troublers, but had not yet beset Israel. The peace and prosperity were deceptive. A couple more decades, and Assyria would begin the destruction of Israel's cities and the mass deportation of upper and middle classes.

The reckoning for ruthless nations

The first stretch of oracles (1.2–2.8) forms a remarkable pattern. From his central throne the Creator speaks judgment on nations around the compass, and finally on the nation at the centre. A similar pattern of world judgment including Israel is found in other prophets (most complete in Zeph. 2.1–3.8). It has some affinity with the customs in the new-year festivals of ancient Egypt. The Egyptians made proclamation of the Creator's sovereignty to the four compass points, and rituals signified doom for trouble-makers over the borders and within Egypt.

The pattern of judgment in Amos 1–2 has probably come from Jerusalem's seasonal festivals, especially that of the autumn, when the sovereignty of Yahweh over his world was freshly proclaimed (Ps. 24, 29, 93 etc). From the Jerusalem temple, mysteriously one with the heavenly throne, Yahweh utters doom like a lion's roar, and the created order feels the impact (Amos 1.2).

'Thus says the Lord' echoes a phrase which was the standard introduction for words entrusted to a messenger ('So-and-so has said as follows . . .'). With this introduction the prophets presented themselves as messengers come from the presence of God. The message begins with the phrase that will be used eight times: 'For three sins of X, and for four'. It is an ancient poetic style, where the rising number – three, four – indicates that even more offences might be added. The refrain each time includes Yahweh's avowal 'I will not cause it to return.' 'It' refers to the divine word that brings punishment; the elliptical style suggests a customary form.

Like an arrow from Jerusalem the first oracle of judgment

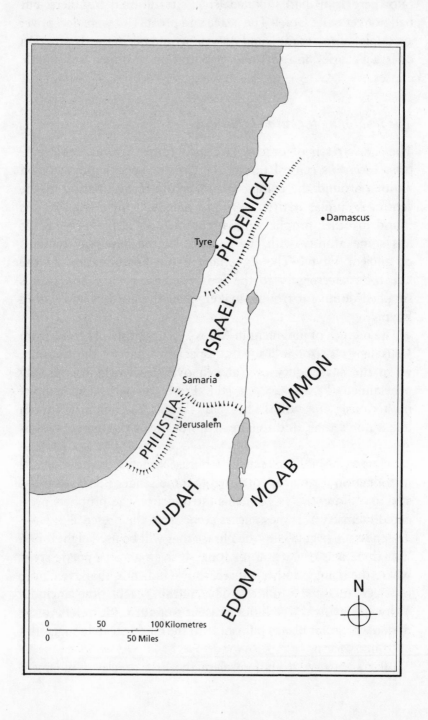

(1.3–5) is aimed over the border to the north-east, to Damascus, capital of the Aramean kingdom – they have ravaged the district of Gilead (near that border) as farmers break corn by drawing over it iron-studded sleds.

The second oracle flies in the opposite direction, striking the Philistine towns in the south-west (1.6–8). They are accused of taking whole village communities to sell as slaves. The third missile of doom flies over the north-west border against the Phoenicians of Tyre (1.9–10). They too have siezed villagers to sell into slavery. In the opposite direction, the south-east, the fourth point of the compass now receives a triple volley of doom, striking at Edom (1.11–12), Ammon (1.13–15) and Moab (2.1– 3), all guilty of ruthless acts. Moab's atrocity violated the feeling that peace after death was associated with the bones; to reduce them to lime was ultimate ruthlessness. The offence was not against Israel, but is condemned all the same.

These acts seemed all the worse since these neighbouring peoples could easily have related mutually in trust and friendship as a family. Old bonds had counted for nothing; brotherly kindness had been violated.

Without a break, the series of doom-words continues, for now it is the turn of those within the borders. Here the first target is Judah, guilty of neglecting the Lord's teaching (*tora*) and preferring lies (false gods) – a charge like that brought by Isaiah (5.24). The terse style suggests that while the pattern had to be completed, the real concern of the judgment was yet to come.

This real concern is finally reached in 2.6. The target is 'Israel', the kingdom centred on Samaria, and its offences are vividly exposed (2.6–8). Through a corrupt parody of justice, the powerful dispossess and enslave the poor. Judges can be bribed for silver (money) and people enslaved for small debts (for a mere 'pair of sandals'). That a father and son have intercourse with the same girl violates a taboo, but also may be an instance of sacred prostitution or of exploitation of the poor, an abuse rife in countries today.

Perhaps it is figurative language when the oppressors are pictured in the long ceremonies of worship reclining on the garments seized as debt-pledges from the poor, and drinking wine exacted as fines – they think to please God with their praises and offerings, but he sees them as brutal and greedy oppressors. Their deeds are ever before his eyes, even as they sing praises.

Later expansions?

In the attempt to distinguish the words of the prophet from the additions made by his successors, some scholars argue that the oracles against Tyre (1.9–10), Edom (1.11–12) and Judah (2.4–5) may be additions made some two centuries later. The charge against Tyre, they argue, only echoes that against Gaza, the charge against Edom suggests the hostilities of a later period, while the charge against Judah is brief and vague and mentions 'tora', a favourite theme of later times.

On the other hand, the pattern of judgment would be deficient without these peoples. Zeph. 2–3 shows how prophets might have only a formal interest in some of the charges; their oracles 'round the compass' built up to what they really burned to say.

A poor reward for the Saviour's love

The Lord's message continues with a contrast: what he has done to give them land and life, and what they have done with these gifts. The nation past and present is seen as a unity; it is this same people brought through perils long ago that is now grieving their Saviour (2.9–12).

Past blessings include the gift of prophets and Nazirites (holy ascetics). Ingratitude for these guides is pinpointed in two little scenes to characterize the general attitude: prophets told to shut up, ascetics made drunk. So, in the day of reckoning, there will be no escape through wealth or technology; the best equipped soldiers will flee away naked (2.13–16).

But the people have made a different use of the story of past salvation. They take comfort from it, assuming continuing protection. Against this, Amos brings a more powerful word

(3.1–2): because of Israel's special place in God's work, she will be held to account for her misdoings. 'You only have I known' is an idiom from Near-Eastern customs of treaties and covenants and means in effect 'I have chosen and appointed you for leadership'. All the greater, then, is the responsibility.

The hearers of Amos could only escape his logic by casting doubt on his inspiration. No doubt there were many other prophets with more comfortable words. As though countering such thoughts, Amos gives some rather ominous examples of how cause and effect belong together (3.3–8). When you hear me, reckon with the lion that has roared from heaven! Before you stands one of 'his servants the prophets' who has heard the roar, and must 'do the work of a nabi' ('prophesy') to convey its message (3.7–8).

The cows of Bashan

Samaria was a fine royal city, laid out on a spacious hill above fertile valleys. With its view of the Mediterranean Sea, it seemed open to the wider world. But here Amos conjures up an amazing scene (3.9–15). The palace-dwellers of Egypt and the Philistine city of Ashdod are summoned to gather on the surrounding hills and be amazed to witness the ill-gotten gains collected in the city and the doom that will fall on her. The only remains of the ruling classes will be the fragments that evidence their end – as a shepherd brings back a bone or two to prove that a sheep has been taken by a lion.

Nor will the chief royal sanctuary, Bethel, be able to offer refuge. The very horns of the altar (the spikes rising at the corners, to which fugitives cling for sanctuary) will be broken off. The rich who have second homes to escape the summer heat will be tracked down. The ivory carvings ornamenting their furniture, being the product of ill-gotten wealth, will perish with the grand houses.

And there is a special word for the powerful women of the capital (4.1–3). The cows of Bashan (a plain near Mount Hermon) enjoy rich pasturage. These women likewise have the best, but are never satisfied. Indifferent to the crushing of the poor, they call to their husbands for more. From the ruined city they will be led in lines to a distant land.

The prophet mounts another attack on the confidence of these wealthy in their piety (4.4–5). At times of festival the horn-trumpets would be blown across the land with the cry, 'Come to Bethel' or 'Come to Gilgal' (a famous shrine near Jericho), 'Come with your offerings and tithes!' Amos adopts the cries ironically: 'Come to Bethel and rebel (against the Lord), to Gilgal and rebel all the more, bring a great show of offerings as you love to do!' The scandal is that oppressors should offer their wealth in the house of God as though he were an associate in their conduct.

Amos now delivers another reading of the past (4.6–11). This time it is the adversities which he picks out – the droughts, plagues, earthquakes. These should have been warnings enough. But now the Lord is to come for a full reckoning: 'Prepare to meet your God, O Israel!' Again the cries and hymns of the festival are used ominously (4.12–13). The expected dawn of his coming for the new year will be turned for these worshippers back into deep darkness, for Yahweh, the Creator, knows their thoughts.

For your research

Collect four different phrases which occur several times each in Amos 1–4. How would you explain such repetition?

A music God hates, and a music he loves

And now something which should appal even a callous people: the prophet chants their funeral dirge, for he has a vision of them already dead (5.1–2) –

> She has fallen, no more to rise,
>   the maiden Israel.
> Prostrate she lies on her land,
>   and none can raise her.

Another visionary picture follows (5.3): of the contingents of militia that leave their towns to swell the army of defence, only a tenth return.

Is there then no hope? Catastrophe is irrevocable. The nation in its present power-structures will be smitten down. But if some of the prophet's hearers yet turn and seek the Lord, they will find life (5.4). They must seek the Lord himself, beyond the corrupted centres of worship; they ·must seek the Creator, humbly acknowledging his sovereign power over stars and skies and waters, and over every human pretence to power (5.5–7).

Some of those listening to Amos have been much concerned with their beautiful homes. These are built, not in the old Israelite style of rough stones packed together and daubed with mortar, but with large blocks chiselled to a perfect fit, a style of which the Phoenicians are masters. The proud owners have also made spectacular vineyards on terracing down the sun-lit slopes. But all these excellent things have been financed by the enslavement of the poor, operated through unjust and ruthless courts. So the owners will not remain to enjoy their splendid facilities (5.10–12).

And in the coming time of disaster, the man of knowledge – perhaps the very one knowledgeable in architecture and agriculture, the one who gives expert advice – he will be dumb amidst the ruins (5.13).

But again a fleeting chance is held out (5.14–15): 'Seek good, and not evil, that you may live!' If they establish justice in the court by the great gates, the festal shout may come true – 'The Lord is with us!' At least some survivors of the Joseph tribes (peopling the northern kingdom) may know his pity.

Yes, survivors are envisaged, but amid fearful losses (5.16–17). Survivors will call to one another to come out and mourn the many dead. In spaces and lanes of the city they will wail and cry *Haw, Haw* (Alas, alas)! And loud too are the lamentations from the fields and vineyards in the vision of the prophet.

Israelites looked forward to the great holy season around the autumnal new year. There was eager expectation of the fresh coming of Yahweh. Making pilgrimage to the temple, the people hoped to be bathed in the light of life (Ps. 36.5–9; 84; 133). And behind the hope of God's coming on the festal day was the hope of a once-for-all-coming, when all would be made well for ever.

The question of hope in Amos

Some scholars are of the opinion that Amos offered no hope. They stress such passages as 'I will not turn back' (2.4, 6) and 'I will not pass by them any more' (8.2), 'no more to rise' (5.1), the parable of the lion, the bear and the snake-bite (5.19), and parts of chapter 9. Looking for strict consistency, they regard the hopeful words in chapter 9 and the gleams in chapter 5 as additions by successors, appropriate after disaster had struck.

Others argue that while Amos was concerned to leave no room for unrepentant optimism, his outlook could hardly have been nothing but destruction. Apart from the positive ending of the book, there are the glimmers in chapter 5 and the following considerations:

1. With his exceptionally poetic and graphic words, Amos seems to aim at persuading, which implies there is still a chance to seek the Lord. *which verses – discuss*

2. His burning concern is the ill-treatment of the poor. It would be a strange justice that would now destroy the lowly with their oppressors.

3. Traditional ideas important to Amos (God's coming to assert his reign, God's special bond with Israel) had a positive aim beyond punishment. *v 2.5 (Exodus) v 14, 15, 18*

All in all, one might conclude that, while Amos came to see the doom of national structures and powerful people as inevitable, he knew that God would build again. It was worth preaching passionately in the hope of saving some for that time.

But Amos sees no joy in store for these worshippers cruel to the poor. For them the day they long for will be terrible darkness, not light. He pictures a man who escaped a lion, then a bear, then reached the house and leaned panting on the wall, relieved at his escape, when a snake disturbed in the crevice gave him a fatal bite So inexorably will their fate pursue them (5.18–20).

[handwritten marginal notes: 5: / 14 / 15 / 6 / 23/24 / 25 / after only / rich are / exiled / (e.g. Exile) / v9 / v9]

But the worshippers have a great organization for appeasing God. Is he not to be mollified by the pilgrimage, the assembly, the wholly burnt offerings, the gifts of produce, the communion meals, the psalms with their beautiful accompaniments of harp and lyre? No, says Amos (5.21–24). All these offerings, being from hands that oppress the poor, God 'hates', he rejects. Rather he would hear the music of the rolling waves of justice, a river of compassion flowing continually in all seasons.

Debate among the prophet's followers

In the prophetic books there are sometimes signs that a radical saying has given rise to much discussion in the circle that preserved the prophet's words.

In 5.25 we may detect reflection on the value of offerings – there was a close relation to God in the wilderness days without such offerings. But in 5.26 there is further reflection, for some traditions spoke of a sacrificial system existing already in the wilderness. So verse 26 takes verse 25 with emphasis on the 'me' – were the offerings for *me?* And it answers, No, they were for the images of the star-deities.

A life of luxury

What is life like for the upper classes in Jerusalem (Zion) and Samaria? Amos sketches the scene at a typical banquet (6.1–6). They recline on couches decorated with inlay of carved ivory, they enjoy music of songs and harps, they drink wine from bowls and smear themselves with costly unguents. And all the while they feel no misgivings for 'the breaking of Joseph' – for breaking up the families of the poor. Leading people they shall continue to be, says Amos, when they go first in lines of captives to be deported (6.7).

A gruesome scene is now portrayed (6.9–10). Ten men have survived catastrophe in one great house, but all die of a plague. Long after, kinsmen come to take out the bones. One calls to another who is in the inmost rooms, 'Are there any more bones there with you?' 'None', he replies, but instantly is silenced by the other, lest he use some pious formula containing the name of God and so call the Lord's attention to their presence in the doomed house. It all points to the weight and persistence of the deadly wrath that is to fall on these grand houses.

Amos searches for ever new ways of bringing his message home, and now presents a riddle: do war-horses charge over crags, or with your oxen would you plough the sea? Here are images of absurd conduct, but no more absurd, unnatural and catastrophic than the perversion of justice in Israel's courts (6.12).

And after the riddle, puns (6.13–14). Alas for those who rejoiced in the victories of King Jeroboam II (II Kings 14.25)! Two towns were captured, Lo Debar and Qarnayim, names which mean 'Nothing' and 'Horns'. 'Boast not,' says the prophet, 'that you have got yourself victorious HORNS – it is NO-THING!' The great extent of territory that Jeroboam has secured will be oppressed by an invader.

For your research

Collect from Amos 5 and 6 evidence as to who were specially addressed in these prophetic speeches. What situations would give Amos the opportunity of reaching such an audience? – *speaking at Shrine in Bethel*

A sensation at Bethel

The followers of Amos have related for us a story of when he prophesied at Bethel. Though only eleven miles north of Jerusalem, this ancient holy place was the chief sanctuary of the northern kingdom. They have placed the story within a climax of visionary experiences recounted by Amos himself. The effect is strikingly dramatic. Amos has set forth three visions, which end by declaring that God's forbearance is over. At this point the high priest calls an end to his prophesying. But somehow (perhaps when he is back in Judah) Amos reveals a fourth vision, confirming the doom of the northern kingdom.

In his account of the visions, Amos relates what Yahweh has 'caused him to see'. Each vision is told in terse prose, and each has the same pattern (7.1–9; 8.1–2). The first vision is of a swarm of locusts. God is preparing it in the time of the spring crops, which give vital sustenance for the long dry summer. In accordance with a traditional work of prophets, Amos intercedes to avert disaster and is successful. The Lord relents. This shall not happen.

Look you!

Like the Welsh, the Hebrew speaker invites you to see for yourself what he describes, to experience anew the scene he once saw. He likes to say *Hinneh!* – 'behold!', 'lo!', 'look!'

So Amos says, 'The Lord Yahweh causes me to see, and look, he's fashioning a locust-swarm . . . and look, he's ordering up a rain of fire . . . and look, the Lord standing above a wall built by a plumb-line, and in his hand there's a plumb-line!'

The second vision is of a rain of fire which the Lord is ordaining to burn up water-sources and fields. But again, at the prophet's intercession the Lord relents.

The third vision is of the Lord checking a wall with a builder's plumb-line. If the wall has moved from true, it will have to be demolished. The message is that the Lord measures the building that is the state of North Israel, the kingdom of Samaria, and he sees it must be demolished, including its great sanctuaries and the dynasty of King Jeroboam II, and this time he will not relent.

So specific a reference to the ruling dynasty is sensational. A kind of *fatwa* against the king, stirring memories of the rebellion and assassinations once launched by the prophet Elisha (II Kings 9)! Amaziah, the priest in charge of this royal sanctuary, has to intervene. But he is torn between fear of the king and caution in face of powerful prophetic words. So he tries a balanced approach. On the one hand he sends a messenger to inform the king, but on the other hand he gives Amos a chance to slip away before the king's orders come back. He could have arrested Amos, but thought instead to put himself in the right either way. It seemed reasonable to direct the Judaean prophet to return and exercise his prophethood in the kingdom of Judah. Amaziah speaks as one who knows Amos, his visionary calling, and his origin in Judah: 'O seer (*hozeh*), hurry, flee to the land of Judah, and there eat bread (i.e. find a welcome, live in peace, perhaps in the brotherhood of sacred orders, where he would be entitled to his portion), and be a prophet there, but here at Bethel prophesy no more, for it is a sanctuary of the king, a temple of this kingdom.'

Amos answers, 'When I was not a prophet, nor the disciple of a prophet, but was rearing cattle and cultivating sycamore fruit, Yahweh took me from behind the flock and said to me, Go, become a prophet to my people Israel.' (Amos begins literally, 'Not a prophet I, and not a son of prophet, and a herdsman I . . . and the Lord took me . . .' For my translation 'I was not . . .' as in the classic translations, as against 'I am not . . .' of some moderns, see also my remarks in chapter 2.) The point is that Yahweh has expressly commissioned Amos to prophesy and to oppose the prophecy is to oppose Yahweh. Even if Amaziah has had some consideration for the prophet's safety, that weighs little against the offence, and Amos delivers a severe oracle against Amaziah and his family – when exile comes, they will suffer first.

In the same spirit of concern only for God's word, the disciples of Amos have not recorded what happened next to their master. Whether in hiding or whether back in Judah, he remained God's nabi, his spokesman, and so what follows is simply his account of a fourth vision, continuing the series, patterned just like the others, and confirming the word of doom

(8.1–3). Truth is conveyed in the Hebrew pun: he sees a basket of end-of-summer fruit (*qayiṣ*) and it means for Israel the end (*qeṣ*). The summer is over for the northern kingdom. Yahweh gets Amos to pronounce the fateful word, and the doom is unleashed.

A fresh address now gives vivid portrayal of behaviour which offends the Lord (8.4–7). Ironically the prophet puts a description of ruthless practice into the mouths of the perpetrators, impatient that the holy rest days have interrupted their unjust trading. The picture is of expanding land-owners who have accumulated the sources of food, depriving the original small-holders, and then exploiting the resultant food trade, 'giving under-weight by the tricks of false measures and weights, and selling chaff and straw'.

From the scene in the market, the prophet's eye turns to the consequences (8.8–13). For the disregard of what is kind and fair, all the earth will be shaken, heaving and sinking like the rise and fall of the great Nile. Day will turn to darkness, festal praise become wailing. People will rush from one great shrine to another, from Samaria in the centre to Dan in the north and Beersheba in the far south. But a word from the Lord will be harder to get than bread in a famine.

The end and the beginning

Whether Amos at some time had the opportunity actually to announce the new-year destiny in the temple at Bethel, or whether the whole scene in 9.1–4 is entirely in the visionary mind, we can hardly tell. But the tense proceedings at the state temple come through vividly.

While the mass of pilgrims worship in the open court, the leading citizens and sacred officials assemble in the relatively small temple building at Bethel to hear the message of the Lord for the new year. His council is sitting in heaven, and destinies are being determined. A prophet is inspired to see the Lord at the head of the council, for the temple is like the threshold of heaven. If all is well, he will see the Lord inaugurate ('crown') 'a year of good' (so Ps. 65.11).

An Egyptian tale of prophecy

From soon after 2000 BCE comes a story about a pharaoh who, centuries before, had desired to be refreshed by a skilful speaker. A priest called Nefer Rohu was recommended and brought to him. Did His Majesty wish to hear about the past or the future?

'If it has taken place by today,' replied the king, 'pass it by.' So Nefer Rohu spoke of times to come – great troubles to be ended by the coming of a good ruler. As he spoke, the king wrote it all down. Here are some lines from the prophecy:

O my heart, how you lament for this land of your origin!
This land is so injured . . . the sun is obscured.
The rivers of Egypt are empty . . .
The south wind blows against the north wind . . .
The pools which used to overflow with fish and fowl are ruined.
People no longer weep because of death . . .
A man's property is taken from him . . .
Though the land is diminished, administrators are many . . .
Deference is shown to one who formerly had to show deference . . .
Those who were under are now on top . . .

Then a king will come from the south . . .
Rejoice, you people of his time!

(For the whole text see Pritchard (ed), *Ancient Near Eastern Texts*, pp.444–46.)

Amos is granted that extra sight to see the Lord presiding 'above the altar'. He reports what the Lord is commanding his servants the angels round about him. It is not good news. It is terrible, for the Lord is saying;

Smite the capitals of this temple
that the very thresholds shake!
Shatter them on the heads of all!
With my sword I will slay any who survive.
Not a fleer of them shall flee away,
not an escaper make his escape . . .

From heaven or hell he will bring them back for judgment. No wonder that the land is not able to bear the force of such words (7.10). If some take refuge in the thought of God's special bond with this people, Amos again has ammunition ready. Does not this Lord of the universe have similar relations with other peoples, such as the Ethiopians, Philistines, and Arameans (9.7)? All he guides, and all, including Israel, he holds to account. And again the sentence is pronounced: this kingdom of Samaria is to be brought to an end (9.8).

But yet beyond all the darkness come glimpses of a new dawn. Though the state organized under the dynasty of Jeroboam is to disappear, along with the oppressive class that it has nurtured, yet something of the true 'family of Jacob' will survive, the people of humble and caring hearts (9.8–10).

And then the amazing collection of prophecies ends with a burst of hope (9.11–15) – whether a disclosure of our prophet's own heart, or whether a perspective which his successors thought right to express, cannot certainly be known. On the one hand, reference to 'the ruins', 'the remnant' and 'the fallen tent of David' could suit a date after 587. On the other hand, the crumbled booth could signify the great reduction of Davidic power after the death of Solomon, while remnants and ruins feature in other visions of Amos.

At all events, this concluding oracle answers to the opening ones, for the great day of the Lord's coming must mean both destruction of evil and establishment of good. In the end, it is for good, for life, that the Creator reigns, and his enduring purpose to reign through this people and the house of David requires fulfilment.

This concluding promise corresponds further to the opening oracles in picturing the former great empire of David as the heart of God's kingdom. For though the opening oracles were like arrows across and all around the borders, the peoples mentioned had all come into David's sphere in his great days. And now it is promised that David's 'hut' or 'booth' (*sukka*) will be repaired – the family of peoples which he had shepherded for God will be made whole again, all the peoples over which the name of Yahweh had once been proclaimed.

The strong feeling for God's kingdom being centred on David's rule from Jerusalem is matched by another strong idea: the unity of people and land. The promise is for a smiling Nature. The vital rainy seasons will come so promptly that preceding work will hardly be completed. Hillsides will flow with juice of the good grapes. Rebuilt villages, vineyards and orchards replanted, and people too planted on their own soil, never again to be uprooted! Such is the promise of 'Yahweh your God', the God of all, but known in intimate, faithful commitment.

For discussion or writing

---

1 – Does the Book of Amos help you to imagine life in town and country in ancient Palestine? Note the features of daily life that he refers to.

2 a – Did Amos have a clear idea of what disaster would shortly befall Israel? Collect passages foretelling disaster and see how far the picture varies.

b – It has been said that Amos had a particular gift for seizing and holding the attention. Note some of the ways in which he achieves this.

[handwritten notes:]

morning sacrifices 4:4
tithes / 3 day / 4:4
some very rich / some poor - rough cut stone
drink wine } agrarian society
eat grain
dangerous animals (5:19)
worship false gods 5:26

2a) Israel - defeated in battle 2:13-16
surrounded by enemy & defeated 3:10,11
breached walls 4:3
shall "fall" 5:2
symbolic - fire, locusts, plumb line, ripe fruit,
broken altar

b) symbolic descriptions - eg cows of Bashan.

THE VOICE OF HOSEA

There is no truth or fidelity
  or knowledge of God in the land.
The solemn swearing is all a deceit.
  There is murder and theft and adultery.
Restraint is cast off
  and one bloody deed succeeds another.

Therefore the land mourns
  and all the creatures that live in it droop,
wild animals and birds,
while the very fish of the sea pass away (4.1–3).

I the Lord delight in faithfulness, not animal sacrifice,
  in knowledge of God rather than whole-offerings (6.4).

They make kings for themselves without reference to me,
  they appoint rulers not of my choice.
With their silver and gold they have made themselves
  idols to their own ruin (8.4).

But you, return into your God,
  keep kindness and justice
    and wait on your God continually (12.6).

How can I give you up, Ephraim,
  how hand you over, Israel?
my heart heaves within me,
  all my compassion is kindled.
I will not execute my anger,
  I will not turn and destroy Ephraim,
for I am God and not man,
  the Holy One in your midst (11.8–9).

Their fickleness I will heal,
  freely I will love them,
    for my anger has turned from them.
I will be as the dew to Israel,
  he shall blossom as the lily (14.4–5).

6

Hosea – Prophet of Divine Compassion

Bible
pg 936

The character of the book

Reading the book for the first time, one must have mixed feelings. It is full of powerful things, but it often seems disjointed. From the prophet's spoken poetry, passages have been remembered, put together in chains, and eventually written down and framed with introduction and conclusion. It now needs patient study to see the point of the sayings against their background, and so appreciate their passionate and spiritual force.

The time and place of Hosea's ministry

From the first verse and from various references to Samaria, Ephraim and the succession of usurping kings (8.4), we can deduce that Hosea was a prophet of the northern kingdom with its capital at Samaria, and that he spoke from the time of the strong king Jeroboam II onwards. His ministry continued into the time of the short-lived kings that led up to the destruction of the state by the Assyrian empire (721 BCE). It was a tragic time, but Hosea found meaning in it all. He told of the people's broken relationship with the Lord, warned of the approaching death of the kingdom, and yet believed that through divine mercy new life would come.

The revival of an ancient cult

Hosea criticized the people especially for their worship of Baal. This deity was the central figure in the religion which had old roots in the area and was still predominant across the borders. He was especially associated with rains and the powers of fertility. He had a consort goddess, and his fertile power over land and people was celebrated and mediated by male and female prostitutes at the shrines.

The beauty of Ephraim and Samaria

When I was living in Jerusalem many years ago, I was always struck on visits to the region of Samaria by the gentler character of the landscape. So in my *Interpreted by Love* (p.95) I wrote as follows:

The city of Samaria was a capital suited to a beautiful land. It crowned a spacious oblong hill with gradual ascent only from the eastern end. From the fine buildings at the western end there was a view to the Mediterranean. The city was surrounded by rich valleys and hillsides. Isaiah (28.1) sang of the grace of its beauty, a proud crown on the head of a valley clad with olives.

The old tribal name of the area was 'Ephraim', meaning 'Fruitful Land'. The kingdom stretched north to the fine mountains of Galilee. The wild flowers, rough stone walls, varied shapes of hill and valley, the wheat, barley, figs, olives and vines delighted the eye in the prevailing sunshine.

All this Hosea knew well. His poetry is full of references to trees, flowers, fruit, crops, scents, dew and mist, rains of autumn and spring. He refers often to the work in field and village, to sowing, reaping, threshing, baking, vintage, and animals and birds.

The religion of Israel's God, Yahweh, had long ago appeared to replace this fertility religion, but there were times when Baal came back strongly. Although it was not a problem that loomed large for Amos, for Hosea, working some twenty years later and with closer knowledge of the northern kingdom, it was a central issue.

The lure of bigger harvests

One factor which increased the appeal of the fertility religion was the desire for extra yield. It was tempting to take this way if it would lead to bigger crops and herds. You might be worried to forego this possible advantage which others were taking. You might be risking your chance of a sufficient harvest and putting your family's welfare in jeopardy. One bad year in that economy was enough to ruin you. So unless faith in Yahweh was strong, the ancient rituals, widespread in the Near East, linked to your landscape and weather, and reviving with all the force of a new fashion, had an alluring appeal.

For your consideration

Why was the promise of Hosea 14.5–7 especially appropriate? *promise of agricultural prosperity*

The subtle erosion of faith

Nor did the religion of Baal always seem a stark alternative to that of Yahweh. 'Baal' was only a title meaning 'Master' or 'Husband', and was in fact sometimes used to refer to Yahweh. Another title of Yahweh was 'Adonay', meaning 'the Lord', and this survived as his chief title; but it was also used for the fertility god, appearing in Greek as Adonis.

And there were other factors of confusion. Most of Yahweh's shrines had been holy places of the earlier religion of Baal. The words for kinds of sacrifices and sacred officers were the same in both religions. Altogether, it was easy to slide into the fertility religion without making a clear decision.

Forsaking all other

Hosea represented the exclusive claim of Yahweh as God other than and above the elements of Nature. According to this traditional Israelite faith (which runs through old stories such as

Ex. 19.5–6; 20.1–6; Josh. 24.14–24; Judg. 6.25–32; I Kings 18.21), Yahweh was the true God who had called the family of Israel to be specially close to him, so as to render him special service. He alone could provide or withold the gifts of life. He was resolute to defend his glory as true God and to claim the exclusive love of his special servants. Hosea's prophetic concern was especially with the bond between Yahweh and Israel, and the fidelity which it required.

He sees such infidelity on Israel's part that he vividly portrays her as Yahweh's adulterous wife. She has gone after her lovers – the fertility gods – in the hope that they will make her rich in food, wool, flax, oil and wine. Individual Israelites are addressed as children of the broken marriage: 'Plead with your mother, plead . . . that she put away her harlotry' (2.2–5). This unfaithful wife and mother brings upon herself such troubles, that she will say, 'I will return to my first husband, for it was better with me then than now' (2.7).

An inscription of King Sargon II of Assyria

For the time of the prophets there is vivid light shed by the Assyrian records and scenic representations. The end of Samaria as Israelite royal capital in 721 is described by the victorious Sargon as follows:

I besieged and conquered Samaria and took away as booty 27,290 inhabitants of it. I formed from among them a contingent of 50 chariots and made the remaining population assume their offices. Over them I set an officer of mine and laid upon them the tribute of the former king.

(For a full text see Pritchard (ed), *Ancient Near Eastern Texts*, pp.284–85.)

How could I give you up?

Hosea did not just denounce the misdirection of worship and faith. He spoke not so much of God's rights as of God's love. He felt intensely the love of God for the people, who were pictured now as God's unfaithful wife, now as his wayward child. He felt the pain of God that his cherished people had become unfaithful, and he came to know that beyond just retribution the love of God would hold on, invincible, and find the beloved again. It was as though Hosea had seen the agonizing struggle in God's own heart, and had been shown, through pain and tears, that the last word was with love.

On the way to this ultimate insight, Hosea was made aware of the depth of the problem. Even when adversity brought a mood of repentance, a desire to return to the Lord and be healed, it was likely to be but a passing phase. The new-found faithfulness was apt to be 'like the morning mist, like the dew that vanishes early'. The true way to God had yet to be found – the way of enduring commitment in a bond of mutual 'knowledge' and love. This was what God valued more than the ritual sacrifices that were supposed to placate him (6.1–6).

Hosea heard God speak also with the heart of a wounded parent (ch. 11). Israel was now seen as the child God loved and saved from sufferings in Egypt. As a mother helps her child to walk and comforts him when he falls, so the Lord had assisted and tended Ephraim (Israel), though the child did not know or care how he was made better. Like a mother, God had led the child on leading strings – bonds of care and protection – and he would lift, caress and gently feed him.

The grown 'son' Israel disregarded all this, forsaking the good parent for worthless idols. So the nation would bring suffering on itself, a new bondage, under new tyrants, and a sword would whirl against the little towns.

Hosea foresaw and probably experienced much havoc that came on his community through the Assyrian invasions. But in all the din of the tragedy he hears these words from the heart of the divine parent (11.8–9):

> How could I give you up, Ephraim,
>   how hand you over, Israel?
> How could I destroy you like Adma,
>   devastate you like Zeboim? (cf. Deut 29.23).

> My heart is overturned within me,
>   my tender love is kindled.
> I will not effect my burning anger,
>   I will not turn to destroy Ephraim,
> for I am God, not man,
>   the Holy One in your midst,
>   and I will not come to destroy.

Beyond the present estrangement and devastation Hosea foresees a new harmony of people, animals and land, when the divine betrothal is made afresh (2.18–20):

> And I (the Lord) will make a covenant for them on that day
>   with the creatures of the wild
>   and the birds of the skies
>   and the creeping things of the ground.

> Bow, sword and battle-line
>   I will break and remove from the earth
>   and I will give you safe repose.
> I will betroth you to me for ever,
>   with dowry of salvation I will betroth you to me,
> with justice, fidelity and tender love,
>   with faithfulness I will betroth you to me
>   and you will know the Lord.

In a communion of all species, one part of creation will respond to another. In this fruitful communion, the Lord, the only source of life, speaks first (2.21–22):

> I will answer the heavens,
>   and they will answer the earth,
>   and the earth will answer the corn, wine and oil
>   and they will answer Jezreel.

'Jezreel' here was a place-name which had been used by Hosea as a symbolic name for his son (1.4–5); it was a sign that God would punish the dynasty for a bloody act committed when it took power. But now the name represents the people in a favourable light, with its original meaning 'God has sown'. It seems that it was to the dynasty of David that Hosea looked in hope of its renewal by God in a just reign over a re-united people (1.11; 3.5).

The relevance of Hosea's marriage

The book contains two somewhat strange narratives about Hosea's family life. These have often been interpreted as the story of an unfaithful wife who was redeemed from degradation by Hosea's persevering love. From this experience, it would seem, Hosea gained his insight into God's persevering redemption of unfaithful Israel. It may be agreed that the prophet's message and his experience of life would be closely connected, but the facts of Hosea's family life remain rather obscure.

Names in old Israel

Names were felt to be of great significance, and a change in fate might require a change in name. The symbolic naming of Hosea's children (1.4–8) and the hope of re-naming (2.1) recalls an incident at a trial in Cairo. A young woman was being tried for theft. 'Stop, your honour!' she cried suddenly. 'Why?' asked the startled judge. 'Because I am in labour,' she replied, and gave birth to a daughter. She at once named the child 'Not Guilty'. The case was suspended.

'Hosea' may be a short form of the name meaning 'Yahweh has saved'.

The first narrative is told about Hosea by his followers (1.2–8). It is related that the Lord directed him to marry a 'woman/wife of prostitution' and from her beget 'children of prostitution' (i.e. children from such a mother). So he married Gomer. As children were born – a son, then a daughter, then a son – the Lord directed him to give them names expressive of judgment on the ruling dynasty and the people of Israel.

Some have suggested that this story's beginning was a 'reading back' – having married normally and then been the victim of infidelity, Hosea came to see the Lord's guidance in his choice of partner. Others think it wiser to take the story as it stands: Hosea performed a prophetic sign comparable with that of Isa. 8.1–4. The phrase 'woman/wife of prostitution' could be taken to mean that Gomer was a prostitute before her marriage, though some think the phrase stigmatized her rather as having had some involvement with the rituals of Baal. At all events, the marriage was part of the sign which culminated in the naming of the children. It is another example of how prophets and their families might walk about as living signs of the divine work, incarnations of the Lord's effective word (cf. Isa. 8.18; Ezek. 12.6). The unchaste woman was a symbol of Israel's infidelity, the specially named children were symbols of the consequences.

The second narrative (ch. 3) is told by Hosea himself: 'And the Lord said to me again, Go love a woman...' Some scholars suggest that this is the same incident as that related in chapter 1, only now in Hosea's version. The 'again', however, points to a fresh incident, and the stories have differing points. One would also think that Hosea's disciples have preserved in chapter 1 an account which the prophet entrusted to them and approved.

If chapter 3 then preserves a fresh incident, who is the 'woman beloved of a companion and an adulteress'? She may be Gomer, whom we must assume to have left home and fallen into bondage. Or she may be another woman, taken as his second wife. But she is not named, and this may point to Gomer.

One cannot be sure, and the fact is that the narrators in these two stories are much more interested in the meaning of the symbolism, in the word that the incidents embody. The first story expresses the estrangement of Israel from Yahweh, while the second reveals the time of austerity which will lead to reconciliation. The circumstances of Hosea and his family remain unclear, but in some way, in folly and sufferings and love, these people were signs for the divine work and witnessed to a judgment that would end in redemption.

For discussion or writing

– Collect and comment on outstanding images in Hosea's poetry.

– It has been said that to bring Hosea close to our world one would have to speak of false goals, the devaluing of faithfulness, and leadership that flatters the people's base instincts. How would *you* relate Hosea's message to modern circumstances?

1:1 harlot wife (unfaithful Israel)
" Jezreel - son
2:5 strip her naked - barren land
lovers - destroy
2:8 thorns - bad crops
bow & sword & war - eliminate

THE VOICE OF MICAH

All the images of Samaria shall be broken to pieces . . .
for from the hire of a harlot she has gathered them (1.7).

Hear you heads and rulers!
Is it not for you to know justice?
You tear the skin off my people
and chop them up like meat for the cauldron (3.1–3).

They build Zion with blood,
Jerusalem with wrong.
Her heads give judgment for a bribe,
her priests give rulings for reward,
her prophets divine to get money.
And yet they lean on the Lord and say
Is not the Lord in our midst?
No disaster can come upon us.
Therefore because of you
Zion shall be ploughed as a field. (3.10–12).

He has shown you, mankind, what is good,
And what does the Lord seek from you,
but to do justice and to love kindness
and to walk humbly with your God? (6.8).

Who is a god like you, taking away guilt?
All our sins you will throw
into the depths of the sea (7.18–19).
In a time beyond time it shall be
that the mountain of the Lord's house
shall stand above other mountains,
raised above all other hills,
and the peoples shall stream to it . . .
He will settle their disputes,
and they will beat their swords into ploughshares
and no longer be trained for war (4.1–3).
From you, Bethlehem, shall come out for me
one whose origins were in the dawn of time . . .
and he will feed his flock
in the majesty of the name of the Lord.
His greatness will reach to the ends of the earth
and he will be their peace (5.1–5).

7

Micah – Scourge of Corruption, Fountain of Hope

Bible
pg 964

The Messenger from Moresheth

Though only seven chapters long, the Book of Micah contains several of the most powerful passages in the Bible. The heading (1.1) introduces Micah as a man from Moresheth (near) Gath (modern Tell-el Judeideh), twenty-five miles south-west of Jerusalem, guarding an approach from the coastal road up to the mountainous region of Jerusalem.

The heading names the targets of his prophecies as especially the two capital cities, Samaria and Jerusalem, and links him with three reigns in Jerusalem – kings Jotham (742–735), Ahaz (735–715) and Hezekiah (715–687). Micah's work may thus have covered a period from the first signs of danger from Assyria (about 736), through the destruction of Samaria (721), to a little beyond the relief of Jerusalem (701). He was probably resident in Jerusalem, where his origin in little Moresheth was remembered as a distinctive trait.

936-701

A great name

'Micah', short for *mi-ka-yah*, meant 'Who is like Yahweh?' Similar is 'Michael' (*mi-ka-el*), 'Who is like God?' It is a very ancient type of name, where the worshipper's gratitude, love and awe well up in such a brief but eloquent testimony to his Lord. The 'Mikes' of today can be glad of their name!

The ministry revealed by the book

The book contains searing words of condemnation, but also positive passages, rising to glorious promises. For some commentators, only the bitter words against injustice in the capitals are to be seen as authentic words of Micah; other materials, especially the promises, are taken to be later than the devastation of 587. But for others, this view is too facile. Micah himself, they suggest, will have addressed over the years a variety of situations and audiences.

Some of the material (such as 6.1–8 and ch. 7) has a form connected with worship. Allowing that even drastic critics of the establishment might be associated with the ministries of worship, we can envisage Micah as having such an association and so ready, at the right time, to follow his words of doom with visions of new glory for the temple and the royal house.

It does not in the end seem possible to decide sharply what words are from Micah directly, and what from his influence on successors. But it is certain that when we hear the book as a whole, we can perceive deep significance in its contrasts. There, precisely there, in the place of utter failure, the new work of grace is done.

The harlot city where money is all

The prophecies begin with an awesome vision of the universal Lord descending in judgment. He aims straight for the centres of wealth and power in 'Jacob' and 'Judah', the twin kingdoms of the covenanted people (1.2–7). As he comes from his heavenly throne, mountains melt, gorges split open, the rocky masses dissolve like wax in the fire or like water cascading down a steep fall.

It all signifies the coming of the power that no human power can withstand. The capital cities of Samaria and Jerusalem, purpose-built to display the ruler's might, cannot escape their doom.

Samaria is here the prime target. The city is pictured as a harlot. She has sold her love for money. Profit has been her all-demanding lover, her ruthless and insatiable god. In the images of her fertility gods and goddesses was the reality of lust for gain and power. Micah has seen through to a greater reality, and brings from the just Lord the message that the fine city will soon be destroyed. The well-cut stones of her prestigious buildings will be thrown down into the surrounding valleys, and only heaps of earth will remain.

The light of justice

From the tablet-library of the seventh-century Assyrian king Ashur-banipal comes a hymn to the solar god Shamash, lightener of darkness, destroyer of evil, faithful shepherd of all on earth and in the Underworld. The concern of this universal god for justice is expressed in such lines as these:

You destroy the horn of the evil-doer.
He who falsifies accounts will be overturned.
A corrupt judge you bring to prison.
He who takes a bribe to pervert justice you punish.
He who refuses bribes and intercedes for the weak
   has the favour of Shamash and gains life.
He who tampers with weights
   acts a lie for profit and will lose.
He who uses the scales honestly gains much.

You listen to prayer.
One who is wretched, needy, ill-treated, poor,
   comes before you trustfully with psalms
     and offerings.
Fearful of the dangers of the wild,
   the shepherd comes before you.
The trader . . . the pedlar . . . the fisherman . . .
   the burglar . . . the vagabond
come before you . . . and you examine their past.
You open the ears of all the world.
For the wings of the glance of your eyes
   the heavens will not suffice.

(For the full text see Pritchard (ed), *Ancient Near Eastern Texts*, pp.387–89.)

Corrupt experts and the butchery of the helpless

Accusation and sentence of Jerusalem are set out more fully in chapter 3. The rulers are condemned for heartless exploitation of the poor. Their treatment of the needy is shockingly described under the figure of butchery – as though they flayed, dismembered and chopped up their victims for the pot.

Micah then directs an oracle against prophets who lead God's people astray (3.5–7). These 'link-persons' (referred to as *nbi'im*, *ḥozim* and *qosmim*) have had revelations, but they abuse their gifts for personal profit. To those who reward them well (giving them 'something to bite their teeth on') they give a favourable message. But to those who do not put sufficient 'in their mouths' they prophesy misfortune. On such manipulators of God's messages the sun of vision will set, the light of divine knowledge will be extinguished.

A further oracle takes in corrupt rulers, priests and prophets (3.9–12). The growth of buildings and property in the capital city has been financed by exploitation of the needy – 'they build up Zion with blood'. Officials, priests and prophets alike exercise their functions for their own gain. And they still assume that they have the Lord's approval, so hardened are their hearts. Because of them, the holy city will become a heap of earth and the temple hill a forest. We have it on record that this terrible word against Jerusalem made a deep impression on the king and led to some repentance and mitigation of sentence (so Jer. 26.16–19).

For consideration

'They lean upon the Lord.' Is the type of leader described in 3.11 recognizable and still to be encountered today?

Am afraid so – corruption, bribes, worship of power (in head of Church)

What the heart has always known

In ancient times, just as today, parties to an alliance or covenant might have procedures for resolving differences. A meeting might be called where grievances could be aired, sometimes in the presence of witnesses.

At the great festivals in old Israel there was likewise an encounter where the relationship of God and people, through frank and solemn speaking, might be repaired. The Lord was understood to draw near in the great assembly, speak critically and sometimes argumentatively through the prophets, and listen to the complaints of his people.

In Micah 6.1–8 we have the outline of such a meeting for 'dispute' (Hebrew *rib*). The witnesses are the surrounding mountains, enduring pillars of earth and sky. But the great Lord of the heavens, in lowly fashion, opens himself to complaint: 'How have I vexed you? Tell me!' There is some irony here, as he reminds his people of examples of the salvation to which they owe their existence. He mentions how he delivered them from slavery and sent great 'link-persons' – Moses, Aaron, Miriam and Balaam – to help them through the desert journey into the promised land.

Whatever grumbles the people came with, the mood now changes. Their thought is rather, 'What shall I render unto the Lord for all his benefits to me?' (Ps. 116.12). But what does the Lord require of them?

With question and answer the wonderful truth is eloquently explained. He is not a god who has pleasure in an ever-rising scale of ritual sacrifice. What he wants is in reality no secret. It has been told to every human heart, and needs only to be heeded in quiet simplicity. It is to

DO JUSTICE (*mishpaṭ,* especially in the care of the needy).

LOVE KINDNESS (*ḥesed,* a friendship that never fails)

AND WALK HUMBLY WITH YOUR GOD ('humbly' or 'attentively').

This simple requirement, of course, they do not find easy to fulfil. In a sense it demands the greatest sacrifice, the sacrifice of themselves. The third part is fundamental. In the devoted walking with their Lord comes the grace to be like him and do his will.

The royal Saviour

In the 'reasoning together' which we have just considered, there is a basis of some hope. God and people *could* yet walk together. We come now to passages where hope is confirmed by great promises of God.

What the gods require

In ancient religions it might be a dread moment when the gods indicated their requirements. The solemnity of the spokesman's pronouncement, in what we would call a highly superstitious society, was overwhelming. Who could stand against it? The requirement in some crisis might be the for the ritual sacrifice of children, sometimes the king's own son (so II Kings 3.27, cf. 16.3 and 21.6). Archaeologists find the remains of infants under foundation stones – dedicatory offerings as in I Kings 16.34. Against this background, how wonderful Micah's teaching about Yahweh's requirements!

Micah 5.1 begins with a time of suffering. The prophet sees invaders assault the capital, Jerusalem. He sees the king illtreated, struck with the very sceptre that betokened his high calling (the shocking event is emphasized with word-play between *shebet* 'rod' and *shopet* 'ruler'). But in verse 2 we hear of another town, the Bethlehem where the royal line of David originated. From this small place, so the prophet declares, God will bring the Saviour, a second, greater David, a star whose rising was appointed in the world's dawn.

The time is appointed, but not yet revealed (verse 3), and the enemies will dominate until the Saviour's mother gives him birth, and the exiles and refugees come back home. The Saviour will be the good shepherd of all peoples, doing the will of God, and in his person embodying God's *shalom* – true life for all creation.

The mountain of the Lord's house

The temple in Jerusalem was seen as a mystery where the heavenly throne and the presence of the Creator could be encountered. And just as there were hopes for the house of David, so there was faith that the full meaning of the holy Presence in the temple would one day be established and revealed beyond all the tragedies of history.

A great oracle to this effect is preserved in Micah 4.1–4, and also in Isa. 2.2–4. It tells of a time when the temple hill will be high above all mountains, a centre of worship for all the world. The weapons of war will be turned into tools of fruitful life, and the peoples will be at peace under the government of God.

Though the temple hill rose above the old city of David, it was still overlooked by surrounding hills (cf. Ps. 125.2). Abroad, there were sacred mountains which towered up to far greater heights. In preferring the hill of Zion (Ps. 48.1–3; 87.1–2; 132.13–14), the Lord shows again how he works with the humble to confound the lofty. But the glory he has given to the lowly will one day be fully evident.

A link between two prophets

The ministries of Micah and Isaiah seem to have covered the same lengthy period and to have been based in Jerusalem. There are similarities in their prophecies, and some have wondered if Micah was a disciple of the great Isaiah. No one can be sure why the oracle of 'the mountain of the Lord's house' comes in both collections, but the circumstance could point to a close association of these two prophets.

A prophet's work in a time of broken trust

Prophets were called to speak *to* God as well as *for* him. Intercessory prayer and bringing God's answer were both considered inspired tasks, and could be joined in the work of one person. Micah 7 is a good example, puzzling at first sight, clear enough when we recognize the changing angles of speech.

On some occasion when the people have assembled at the sanctuary, Micah begins by lamenting to God the state of society (7.1–7). Like vines denuded after harvesting, so the earth is denuded of faithful people. Aggression, corruption and betrayal run through the public scene and into the heart of family life. The prophet presents it all to God and waits and works for him to respond.

A warning against trust

Pharaoh Amen-em-het I (died about 1960 BCE) is said to have cautioned his successor as follows:

Keep apart from your subordinates . . . do not approach them in your loneliness. Do not fill your heart with a brother, do not know a friend, do not make yourself intimates. Even when you sleep be your own guard, for no one can count on supporters when trouble arises. I gave to the needy and reared the orphan, but he whom I fed raised troops against me.

(For the full text see Pritchard (ed), *Ancient Near Eastern Texts*, p.418.)

Psalms of lament often included a statement of confidence in God's hoped-for help. In similar fashion the prophet now voices on behalf of the congregation confidence that they will be delivered; after well-merited suffering they will see the downfall of the invaders (7.8–10). He then goes further, giving to Zion a message of coming glory – 'a day for the building of your walls . . .' (7.11–13).

Again as in the Psalms, God's promise is followed by a prayerful response: 'Shepherd your people with your staff . . .' (7.14–17). Then the whole interchange is concluded by an expression of confidence in God's mercy (7.18–20): 'Who is a god like you . . .? You will cast all their sins into the depths of the sea; you will deal truly with Jacob and keep faith with Abraham, as you swore to our fathers from the days of old.'

The passage discloses to us a prophet accustomed to take the lead in national gatherings for worship, able to alternate his speech, now for God, now for the people. He was strong in seeing the sins of his society, but dedicated also to a work of mediation. He condemned, but he also interceded for his wayward people, and in time was able to bring back words of grace.

For discussion or writing

– Beside Micah's summary of the Lord's requirements (6.8) we can put Hos. 12.6:

> But what you must do is to
> return into your God,
> keep kindness and justice.
> and wait on your God continually.

Compare the two summaries and consider which you prefer. *I like Micah - proactive*

– What do you think are the most significant points in the promises given in the Book of Micah?

THE VOICE OF ISAIAH

An ox knows his owner, a donkey where his master feeds him.
   Israel does not know, my people has no sense (1.3.)

When you stretch out your hands, I will veil my eyes from you.
   Though you multiply prayers, I will not hear,
     for your hands are covered in blood.
Wash and get clean,
   take from my sight the evil of your deeds!
Cease to do evil, learn to do good,
   follow justice, undo cruelty,
stand up for the fatherless, take up the widow's cause!
                    (1.15–17).

Flee into caves, hide under the ground
   away from the terror of the Lord, the splendour of his majesty!
Abased shall be man's haughty eyes,
and human pride brought low,
   and on that day the Lord alone will be exalted (2.10–11).

Woe to those who call evil good and good evil,
   offering darkness as light and light as darkness,
   bitter as sweet and sweet as bitter! (5.20).

In returning and rest you will be saved,
   in stillness and trust shall be your strength (30.15).

Every trampling jack-boot and the uniforms stained with blood
   are only for burning, just fuel for the fire,
for a Babe is born for us, a Son is given to us,
   and the sovereignty shall be on his shoulder.
And he names him Wonderful Counsellor,
   Divine in Strength, Enduring Father, Prince of peace
                  (9.2, 5, 6).

Wolves will lodge with lambs,
   and leopards will lie down with kids,
and calves and lions will feed together,
   and little children will mind them (11.6).

8

Isaiah – The Greatest

An amazing book

From all the surprising discoveries in the caves of the cliffs overlooking the Dead Sea, none is more impressive than the fine scroll of the Book of Isaiah from near the time of Jesus. This is appropriate, since it is the greatest of the prophetic books – in size, in poetic brilliance, and in the range of its vision and message.

It is fairly clear that the 66 chapters contain strata deposited by several centuries of prophetic activity. The background of chapters 40–55, for example, is Babylonia around 550–540 BCE, two centuries after Isaiah's call. Most of chapters 56–66 reveal circumstances a little later still, just after the end of the Exile.

The prophet Isaiah's own voice can be heard in many of chapters 1–39, though even in these chapters some of the material, especially much of 24–27, is commonly thought to be from a later time. There are narratives *about* the prophet in chapters 7, 20, and 36–39, while Isaiah himself recounts his experiences in 6 and 8. The narratives in 36–39 have parallels in II Kings 18.13–20.11, while the famous oracle in 2.2–4 occurs also in Micah 2.1–3. Fresh headings (as in 1.1; 2.1; 13.1) point to the joining of collections.

There is thus a long history of compilation behind the book, which has evidently grown in stages. All the more remarkable then, is the coherence of the book's themes. There is an all-embracing sense of a purpose of God in history, along with the call to bear faithful witness to it. There is a recurring expectation of the showing forth of the holiness and royal glory of God, to judge and save. There is continuing abhorrence of worship without justice. Often thought concentrates on a remnant, a foundation stone, a seed, a root, the holy city, the royal Servant, and often again the view widens to a vision of healing light for all peoples and creatures. The very title of God as 'the Holy One of Israel' is far more frequent here than in any other Old Testament book and occurs in all the main strata – a clear sign of continuity.

In some way, then, we have to reckon with a ministry which not only left a very substantial deposit, but also bequeathed an influence which affected later contributions to the book. This influence may be readily understood in terms of the Near Eastern systems of disciples, chains of committed people who learn, preserve and develop the master's teaching through several generations. As it happens, an important passage (8.16–22) can be taken as an account of the solemn commissioning of such a group of disciples. They are to be witnesses to Isaiah's teaching as they serve at the great religious centre as guides to the people. We shall have to reckon with them again when we study chapters 40–55. Eventually, of course, the material will have been handled by more general scribal circles, but it did not lose its character as a tradition of Isaiah and his followers.

Isaiah's role

In one of the most famous and fruitful passages in the Bible, Isaiah relates how he offered himself for the Lord's service (ch. 6). That happened 'in the year that King Uzziah died', 642, when a reign of forty years in Jerusalem, an era of strength and prosperity, came to an end. Already there were signs of danger looming up for the two Israelite kingdoms, as Assyria found fresh opportunity to expand its empire westwards. It was a time when prophetic souls might be sensitive to great works of God in his world, and might look penetratingly at the moral and religious state of the nation.

Isaiah was probably then quite young, as there were forty years of his ministry still to unfold. He will have had some knowledge of the work of Amos. Like Amos, he had poetic gifts enriched by education and 'wisdom', the reflective learning, rich in proverb and parable, which formed the basis of schooling. He was in fact to be one of those prophetic guides that kings would consult or have to listen to, guides giving practical counsel in times of crisis.

The situation of his call in the temple (with such details as altar, tongs and brazier) combines with other indications to suggest that he was a prophet of the kind that was associated with the sanctuary and its worship. There is his theme of God's holiness, and the corresponding sense of human defilement and need of purification and atonement. At the time of the festive sacrifices he is there, able to interpret the mood of God. He has much to say about the destiny of Zion and the prospects for the royal house.

And then there is his wife, whom he simply calls 'the prophetess' (*nbi'a*), his children to whom he gives symbolic prophetic names (7.3; 8.1–4), and his disciples who are a group that pilgrims would approach with requests for divination (8.16–21). His prophecies have been handed down with some interweaving of psalm-like passages (chs.12; 25; 26; 33), suggesting a link with gatherings for worship. And like Jeremiah and Ezekiel, he sometimes uses the traditional prophetic method of symbolic action (Isa.8; 20).

Altogether, we are led to think of the prophet living and working at the centre of the national religion, Zion, bringing messages to kings and congregations, consulted by high and low, associated with other prophetic men, women and disciples, familiar with rites, symbols and healing arts (38.21). At times he launches devastating criticism, but at other times he points the way out of danger, and even tells of divine salvation beyond disaster. Prophesying such ultimate salvation, he fulfils his own name, which means 'Yahweh has saved', or 'Yahweh is salvation'. It is in this perspective of God's will to save that the great book which developed from his work came to be so highly treasured.

I saw the Lord

Isaiah's account of his call is indeed an extraordinarily rich passage (ch. 6). The details are carefully given, no doubt to reinforce the message that emerges. We are meant to understand that here is a divine revelation that cannot be treated lightly.

With the end of a great royal era, the entranced prophet sees the true and eternal king, for whom human kings are but servants. Heaven is manifested in the temple. The Lord's high throne thus appears above the ark in the Holy of Holies, the inner room where the divine Presence was symbolized. The Lord himself is not described – only that his flowing robes roll down and fill the main temple hall, the nave, conveying the sense of the dominating Presence. Robes and throne point already to a solemn moment in the divine kingdom, a time of decision and destiny, a new beginning as glimpsed in the rites for the new year (cf. Ps. 93 and 99).

Fiery angelic beings, 'seraphim', attend upon the heavenly king, ascribing to him alone godhead and divine majesty. They chant this tribute responsively and declare that this unique 'holiness' and 'glory', as it were the aura of the One who now shows himself, is so great as to fill the whole world. The foundations of the temple are shaken by the noise of this mighty hymn, and the smoke of the incense of the heavenly worship fills the building. Isaiah then describes how he cried out in lament at his unworthiness to see the Creator-King, for he was polluted by his own sins and those of his people. Surely he must perish! But one of the seraphim flies to the altar of incense and with the priest's tongs takes a burning coal and with it touches Isaiah's lips So his sin is purged and expiated, and his lips in particular are ready for the service of God.

At that moment he hears the voice of the Lord addressing his heavenly court, consulting them and asking who will undertake his errand. Isaiah offers himself: 'Here am I, send me.' The spatial identity of the heavenly palace and the temple is particularly clear now, and there is also an interesting contrast with Moses (Ex. 4.10–13) who said 'Please send some other person', and Jeremiah who said 'I am but a child' (Jer. 1.6).

So Isaiah is comissioned and given the message of destiny for his people. The message foresees estrangement from God their Saviour, and when Isaiah looks for some mitigation (6.11), he is given the prospect of ruined cities and exiled people. Only at the very end does the message, in a rather enigmatic way, glimpse the possibility of a new beginning after the ruin.

Religious awe in Assyria

Praise of a god 'exalted in his uniqueness' was written on a tablet in Nineveh soon after Isaiah's time, but copied from an older text. The god of the moon (Sin=the Sumerian Nanna) was here identified with a primitive father of the gods (Anshar) and the god of heaven, chief of all the gods (Anu). Here are some extracts:

O womb giving birth to everything,
  dwelling with living creatures in a holy residence,
Begetter, merciful and forgiving,
  holding in your hand the life of all the
      earth,
Lord, your divinity fills with awe the broad
      sea,
  the farthest heavens also.
Namer of rulers, bestowing the sceptre,
  appointing destiny to far-off times,
great prince whose deep heart none of the
  gods can comprehend . . .
opening the door of heaven and giving light
  to all people,
who is exalted in heaven but you alone?
Who is exalted on earth but you alone?
When your word alights on earth the green
  things grow.
Your word brings into being truth and justice
  so that the people speak truth.

(For the full text see Pritchard (ed), *Ancient Near Eastern Texts*, pp.385–86.)

There is something mysterious, too, about the core of the commission. Literally, it seems that Isaiah is to preach repentance in order to harden hearts and ensure that they do not repent and be healed. There may be reference here to the fact that those who are shown a good way and despise it are then only hardened in their evil. But perhaps the main key to the passage is to recognize its irony, a bitterly sorrowful irony. Isaiah is thus in effect commissioned to call his people to turn again to the Lord and be healed, but he is warned that there will be ever less receptivity to the word of the Lord. Ears will not listen, eyes not perceive, hearts will grow ever more callous, until disaster engulfs the communities of Israel.

How does the great chapter hold together as a unity? How does the hymn to God's holiness relate to the prediction of doom? One can see a connection between the holiness of the Lord and the fate of the people that takes an unholy way, and one can note that the final words enigmatically glimpse a redeeming holiness.

But the unity of the account can best be grasped if we see the prophet's experience entirely in the context of worship. Study of the holy season of the autumnal new year and 'Tabernacles', especially with regard to psalms like 93 and 96–99, has indicated that the main theme was the kingship of God. The ceremonies represented a dramatic manifestation of Yahweh as Creator-King, high above all powers. He came with judgment, assessing his people and making decrees for the new year. Worship in the temple united with that of heaven, as all above and all below together cried 'Glory!' (Ps. 29.9) and ascribed holiness, divine supremacy, to Yahweh alone (Ps. 99.3,5,9, a three-fold formula).

It seems that it was at this festival that Isaiah was carried beyond normal perceptions to see and hear sharply the reality beyond the symbols. He saw the exalted King of All, vividly knew the unity of the temple and heaven in worship, and was present in the heavenly council. Here he knew himself commissioned with a message for the new year, the decree for 'this people' (6.9, 10), this assembly that waited for announcement of their new-year fate. But alas, the message was not like that of Psalm 85.8–13, a message of *shalom*; the Lord was not 'installing' a 'year of his favour' (Ps. 65.11). The message was that this and the future years were heading for disaster.

Reigns in Jerusalem

Uzziah	783–742
(with Jotham co-regent from 750)	
Jotham	742–735
Ahaz	735–715
Hezekiah	715–687

Isaiah's advice in a local war

We hear of Isaiah's activity especially in three political crises. The first of these was early in the reign of King Ahaz. A narrative in chapter 7 tells us how the kings of (northern) Israel and of Syria joined forces to invade Judah, and fear swept through Jerusalem like a gale through the forest. The aim of the invaders was to depose the king because he was unwilling to join their coalition against the threat from Assyria.

Meeting Ahaz by the waters that flowed gently from the spring Gihon to the pool of Siloam, Isaiah brought counsel of quiet trust: 'Take heed and be quiet, fear not, nor let your heart be faint . . . If you do not firmly believe, you will not be kept firm and secure.' The king, however, had his own plan – to volunteer tribute to the Assyrian king and so ensure his speedy assistance. Isaiah saw this as lack of faith in the Lord's protection.

With Isaiah stood his little son, symbolically named 'Shear Yashub' (A Remnant shall Return). There was mystery here. Was it doom (only a remnant would be spared) or hope (beyond disaster a remnant would return to God and be blessed)?

Mysterious too the famous prophecy of Immanuel (7.10–17). A young woman is to bear a son and call him 'God is With Us'; in a matter of months, that is, Judah will celebrate deliverance from

Some details on the sign of Immanuel

It is often pointed out that the Hebrew *'alma* used in 7.14 means not specifically 'virgin' (*parthenos* in the pre-Christian Greek translation, followed by Matt. 1.23) but more broadly 'young woman'. And it is sometimes concluded that Isaiah intended no more than a time reference for a change of fortune – within months God would remove the invaders.

But it is likely that more is involved. The prophet's words are reminiscent of utterances in neighbouring countries foretelling divine salvation through a royal birth. Then there is a text from the north Syrian coast (from Ras Shamra, ancient Ugarit, before 1400 BCE) which has almost the same formula as Isaiah – 'Behold, the *ǧalmatu* (=Hebrew *'alma*) will bear a son' – and refers to a lunar goddess, whose happy fate is being desired for a human bride. In much later times (third century BCE) and living in Egypt, the Jews who put their scriptures into Greek were sensitive to the overtones of divine solemnity and marvel in the enigmatic prophecy, and so rendered, 'Behold the maiden (*parthenos*) shall conceive and bear a son'.

Isaiah himself will have drawn on traditions that focussed on God's reign through the royal house. The invaders were out to replace the Davidic king, but Isaiah has a word of potential salvation, evocative of God's purpose through David. With the *'alma* then, Isaiah thought of the queen: through her and her promised child God would confirm and renew the royal house, offering divine peace and salvation. The 'curds and honey' (7.15), a divine food in various ancient traditions, also point to a divine work (perhaps involving a time of tribulation when the child would not have the mother's milk).

Isaiah's hearers would sense the solemnity and mystery. The 'sign' was a summons and an encouragement to faith. Working through the Davidic dynasty, God would come with salvation, if only there were faith and humility.

(The Ugaritic text is presented in Gibson's *Canaanite Myths and Legends,* pp.30–31, 128–9.)

the invaders. The young woman is referred to in a way that suggests a well-known figure, and the Greek translators seem to have been aware of a special background when they rendered the term as 'the virgin'. The mystery is deep, especially as we note the following predictions of strange circumstances, some blissful, some ominous. The likelihood is that the whole prophecy of Immanuel connects with an ancient Near Eastern poetical tradition (as recognized for example by Ringgren in *The Messiah in the Old Testament*, pp.25–27). Taking up the ancient phrases and motifs, and referring probably to a coming royal child, Isaiah not only tells of an early military deliverance, but hints at a wonderful salvation, messianic times which are so near, ready to break like morning, if only king and people will trust the Lord. As the crisis developed, Isaiah performed a symbolic action to convey God's doom upon the invaders from Damascus and Samaria (8.1–4). But further oracles condemned also the persistence of Ahaz in his reliance on Assyrian intervention (8.5–22). It was at this early stage of his ministry that Isaiah gave his disciples the task of witnessing to the Lord's guidance, in opposition to a people ready to trust anything but their true helper (8.19–22). Though he saw dark days ahead, he would not abandon his witness and work for the light.

For your research

'The Lord will shave with a razor that is hired' (7.20). Can you find five more such striking images in chs. 6–8?

The sign of the naked prophet

Assyria soon attacked the states of Syria and Northern Israel. After a further decade of precarious survival, Samaria itself was taken (721). But the subject states of western Asia were ever looking for opportunities to rebel. They conspired together and with the Egyptian empire.

Isaiah counselled King Hezekiah not to put any trust in such alliances. His poetry gives vivid impressions of the Nile Valley and its swarms of insects, the tall smooth Sudanese or Nubians who were ruling the Egyptian empire, and the ambassadors sailing swiftly in their reed skiffs along the Nile (28.1–2). And over all this busy scheming the Lord, serene in his control of the world, looks down, silent and still as shimmering heat or a high cloud of mist, yet ripening his plan to the right moment for action (18.4–5).

Prominent in the rebellion was the Philistine city of Ashkelon. Eventually, in 711, the Assyrians took the final measure of destroying the city and deporting the inhabitants. Around this time, Isaiah went about unclothed for three years in imitation of a captive of the Assyrians. It was prophetic symbolism to foretell the doom of the Egyptian empire and to reinforce his counsel that Hezekiah should not take part in these schemes (ch. 20). The drastic action illustrates the total dedication of the prophets. It seems that Isaiah normally wore 'sack(cloth)', the rough hair garment that may have been the hall-mark of the nabi's calling (II Kings 1.8; Zech. 13.4; Mark 1.6).

A lodge in a garden of cucumbers

When Sennacherib acceded to the Assyrian throne in 705, he faced rebellion from Babylon and also from Judah and some Philistine cities. Only in 701 was he free to invade Judah, but then he made short work of all the towns except Jerusalem. The destruction was terrible. His own annals put the number of stormed cities and fortresses in the little kingdom at forty-six. Isaiah spoke of cities burnt down, produce consumed by the invaders, Jerusalem solitary like a watchman's hut on the hillsides of the vineyards, a disaster little short of the famous cataclysm that had wiped out Sodom and Gomorrah (1.7–9).

But, amazingly, Sennacherib left Jerusalem and King Hezekiah to survive. He accepted submission and a heavy tribute and departed. For one reason or another he had found it expedient not to prolong his campaign further.

Corresponding to Sennacherib's own account, we have a concise report of these events in II Kings 18.13–16. But in addition there is an exciting and colourful version of Jerusalem's escape in II Kings 18.17–19.37, itself thought to combine two accounts (this is the version given also in Isa. 36–37). While this colourful version is not usually accepted nowadays as plain history, it may preserve details which Sennacherib had no interest in recording. Certainly it shows how Isaiah was remembered for his fearless and powerful oracles in a supreme crisis.

Extracts from Sennacherib's annals

As Hezekiah the Jew did not submit to my yoke, I besieged 46 of his fortified towns and stormed them with ramps and battering rams . . . and drove out 200,150 people . . . and horses, mules, donkeys, camels, large and small cattle without number as booty.

Him I made prisoner in his royal city Jerusalem like a bird in a cage . . . I reduced his territory but increased his annual tribute . . . he sent me later to Nineveh 30 talents of gold, 800 of silver, precious stones, couches and chairs inlaid with ivory, elephant hides, ebony . . . and his daughters, concubines, male and female musicians.

(See further Pritchard (ed), *Ancient Near Eastern Texts*, p.287.)

There are other chapters in Isaiah where the prophet's involvement in the crisis is reflected. We see again how he opposed Judah's policy of planning rebellion with other states. Against the scornful leaders he held out the prospect of ruin, because they did not trust in the Lord and wait quietly on him (28.14–22). To send to Egypt for help was to trust in human weapons (31.1–4). In returning to God and resting in him, in quietness and faith, lay the way of salvation (30.15).

Isaiah saw Assyria as the instrument of God's judgment (10.5). But he also saw that this instrument boasted itself above its user, the axe boasted itself above the hewer (10.7–15). So the Assyrian would fall in turn by a sword, not of man (31.8), while the Lord would come down to protect Zion like the flying down of birds (31.5). When the Assyrians withdrew, some citizens of Jerusalem were jubilant, but Isaiah saw the suffering of all the nation and remembered the folly that had caused it, and he rebuked the revellers (22.1–14).

In the footprints of Isaiah

Many archaeological discoveries and thrilling decipherments of strange scripts have given us knowledge of life and history in the ancient Near East. For Isaiah's time we have not only the detailed though selective accounts of the invasions of Palestine from the Assyrian royal annals, but also the almost photographic representations by the Assyrian war-artists, who carved the scenes of conquest on stone slabs to adorn Sennacherib's palace. Especially interesting is the scene of the capture of Lachish, a great Judaean fortress town which fell in 701 (cf. II Kings 18.14) and which has been thoroughly excavated.

Also from Isaiah's time we have the important Hebrew inscription from the rock inside the tunnel that Hezekiah had hewn under Jerusalem to lead water from the spring Gihon to a reservoir within the city (Isa. 22.9, 11). This inscription was only 25 feet from the southern end of the tunnel, but it remained undiscovered in the darkness until noticed by some boys bathing there in 1880.

A sepulchre which gave Isaiah great offence (22.15–25) may have been identified through the skilful decipherment of its damaged epitaph in 1953. It is one of the ancient tombs on the rocky slope where the Arab village of Silwan (=Siloam) is perched, across the valley from the Gihon spring. It has a rock-cut chamber and a dressed facade with a door over which the epitaph was carved.

(See further Wright, *Biblical Archaeology*, pp.164–72; Frank, *An Archaeological Companion to the Bible*, pp.191–99.)

Ah, sinful nation!

The records of Isaiah dealing with policy-makers in times of national crisis have shown us much of his teaching about the life with God, boldly applied to practical situations of war and diplomacy. But the book also contains rich deposits of his prophesying in Jerusalem in a more general way, especially his messages of social criticism in the name of the Lord.

There are powerful examples in chapter 1. Lacking the wisdom of the ox and ass, this people do not remember who has cared for them, given them all they have. Their corrupt deeds are at bottom a forsaking of their Lord, a despising of the God who showed his divine power and love especially in this people Israel. Worship of a kind is not lacking, far from it. But, offered by a people stained by heartless deeds, it is disgusting to God. Especially those in authority are at fault. Swayed by love of profit and plain bribes, they disregard the rights of the unprotected, the vulnerable widow, fatherless and immigrants.

But just as Isaiah worked positively for his people in political dangers in spite of his foreseeing doom, so in his moral denunciations he would at times point to a good way still open: 'Wash and make yourselves clean . . . learn to do well, relieve the oppressed . . . though your sins be as scarlet, they shall be white as snow.'

In chapter 2 we hear another theme of criticism. It seems that with the thrust for commercial gain old but vital values have been swamped. International trading has brought in alien practices of sorcery and idol worship. Hearts are set on silver and gold, and prestigious horse-drawn chariots, and people bow down to things their own hands have made. There is pride in possessions and military constructions, but on the Day of the Lord, the decisive time of judgment, such pride will be brought low and Yahweh alone will be exalted.

In chapter 3 Isaiah foretells a time when the ruling class will be removed, though social anarchy will follow. In the meantime he continues to rebuke the princes and elders: 'What do you mean by crushing my people, grinding the faces of the poor?' Like Amos, he notes the contributions of the rich and vain women to the society of greed and injustice. Lavishly provided with all the equipment of self-adornment, they walk in the city vainly and even wantonly: 'The daughters of Zion are haughty and walk with stretched-up necks and wanton eyes, with mincing steps and tinkling anklets.'

Chapter 5 begins intriguingly. It is like a wedding scene. Yahweh is the bridegroom and Israel or Zion the bride. The prophet is the best man, the groom's friend, who on the groom's behalf sings a song in praise of the bride. At least, the song begins as though in praise and compares the bride to a beautiful vineyard. What care the groom has given to his chosen one! But then the song startles by passing to the groom's bitter disappointment. For all his love and trouble, the vineyard has yielded not sweet grapes, but sour. No one would blame him for finishing with his vineyard.

The idea of this parable may have arisen in the great autumn festival, when the Lord came to Zion like a bridegroom to his beloved bride. The expected song of love has been replaced by one of rejection, because Yahweh looked for the fruit of *mishpaṭ* (justice) but behold, *mispaḥ* (cruelty); he looked for *ṣedaqa* (fair-dealing) but behold, *ṣeʿaqa* (a cry of pain).

The wealthy are depicted as never satisfied, for ever swallowing up the properties of others, despising their ancestral rights (5.8). Rather ironically, Isaiah pictures revellers who rise early to run after liquor; late at night they feast with drink and music, but have no thought of the works of God (5.11–12). He tells of those who draw loads of sin as with cart-ropes, for they mock prophecies of God's action: 'Let him hasten his work for us to see,' they cry, 'let the purpose of the Holy One of Israel come near for us to know it!' (5.18–19).

The prophet laments the deliberate distortion of values. So slick at self-justification, these leaders of society call evil good and good evil, and put darkness for light and light for darkness. They are truly great when it comes to drinking and to taking bribes to acquit the guilty (5.20–23).

There are prophets (*roʾim* and *ḥozim*), like Isaiah's own circle, who offer good guidance from the Lord. But their challenging, critical words are not welcome. Deceitful prophecies that flatter ruthless ambitions and greed are all that are wanted (30.9–14).

For writing or discussion

The *Tao Te Ching,* ascribed to Lao Tzu, is a classic and still favourite text of only eighty-one little paragraphs from ancient China. It often has advice for governments, particularly that they should not be intrusive and aggressive. Success will not result from their own ambitious show of force, but from quietly seeking the ultimate values and letting the Way (Tao) that is ultimate and infinite do its work through them. By such stillness all can be accomplished. To trust in human force is to be weak. Weapons are manifestations of fear. A fish that stays in deep waters is safe, and so is a country that quietly rests in the Way, the ground of all being, the all embracing. Follow Heaven's Way, and the country will be saved without reliance on human force.

Can you present Isaiah's counsel to rulers in a way that would make sense to Chinese teachers? Helpful translations of the *Tao Te Ching* include those of Arthur Waley, Lin Yutang and Martin Palmer.

Visions of a better world

We have already seen that, though Isaiah from the outset looked realistically into the depth of human wickedness and the ruin it must bring, he never ceased to show a positive way, urging return to the Lord in trust and quietness and compassionate justice. This positive aspect appears still more strongly in prophecies of hope for the lineage of David and the sanctuary of Zion. Here we meet belief in the Lord's purpose to establish through these means a divine kingdom, a world of right order and peace.

The relevant passages (2.2–4; 9.1–7; 11.1–9; 32.1–5; cf. 7.1–17) are sometimes judged to be later than Isaiah, suiting better the time when the monarchy was no more. But it may be wiser to allow that this theme, so strongly represented in the book, was part of Isaiah's own faith. From the Psalms and from ancient Near-Eastern sources we can see that the role of royal rulers and temples was interpreted with visionary ideals already in their own day. For Isaiah and other poet-prophets around the temple it was not just a matter of brooding about a far-off perfect world, but of knowing that as God was near, so also was the possibility of the fulfilment of his purpose. The approach of the perfect kingdom of the Lord was indeed in the mind of all the worshippers in the climax of the autumn festival. But seers like Isaiah were caught up in the vision of it, and remained for ever aware of what they had seen.

It is likely that the prophecy of 9.1–7 was made at a royal ceremony, either an enthronement or the investing of a new-born prince as heir to the throne. After a prediction in verse 1 that three northern areas annexed by Assyria in 734–32 will be restored to Israel, the main poem begins. Thanks are here given on behalf of the community that the suffering people has now seen a great light. God has decreed an end to foreign oppression and given a Davidic heir who will reign in salvation. Special names have been given by God to this heir, indicating the triumph, compassion and plenty of his reign – Marvellous Strategist, Mighty Warrior, Father For Ever, Bountiful Ruler. So the reign of David through his descendants, in justice and goodness, will grow and ever continue.

But in 11.1–9 we first see only the remnant of the great dynastic tree, only the tree-stump. Yet this is still well-rooted in the ground, and may signify the royal house humiliated, but not yet torn away into exile. From the stump, says the prophet, and from the roots, a new shoot will grow and blossom. A new David will arise, powerful through the gifts of the Spirit to mediate God's kingdom of peace and justice. With evil purged, a gentle love will envelop all species. The holy mountain of Zion is the centre of this peace. There the Saviour of David's line reigns beside the Presence of God, and from there the knowledge of God (communion and close relationship with him) flows out to cover the world. This is the centre for all peoples (cf. 2.2–4), the source of revelation and rule for a world of peace.

In 32.1–6 the prophet envisages both the righteous king and also the princes and administrators who serve beneath him. Through the justice of their rule the people will find relief from their sufferings, like shelter from the tempest, like water in the desert, like the shade of a great rock. It will be a realm of healing and happiness.

Chapter 7, as we have seen, shows how in specific a crisis Isaiah tried to share his strong faith in the promises of God to the House of David. We noted how, in his predictions of an end to the invaders within a few months, he hinted also at a great outbreak of divine salvation. The time when, through a descendant of David, people would say 'Immanuel – God is with us', that time was a light in the prophet's soul, making hope a very near thing, inspiring him to minister through the tragedies of many years.

In later legends it was said that Isaiah was martyred in the reign of Manasseh (cf. II Kings 21.16). We can believe that he remained to the end a man firm in faith and hope. How wonderfully his prophetic voice has come down to us! How uplifting still his visions!

For discussion or writing

– Can we fairly describe Isaiah as an early kind of pacifist?

– How would you understand the commission given to Isaiah in chapter 6? And how would you relate it to the promises in chapters 9 and 11?

6:10 – action to do

9 result

11 eventual peace/prosperity

THE VOICES OF NAHUM, HABAKKUK
AND ZEPHANIAH

Who can stand before his indignation,
  in the heat of his anger who can remain?
His fury streams out like fire,
  the rocks are riven at his approach.
Yet the Lord is good,
  a stronghold in the day of distress,
    he cares for those who shelter in him (Nahum 1.6–7).

Lord, how long must I cry for help
  and you will not hear,
how long cry 'Murder!'
  and you will not rescue?
Why make me see such evil,
  witness such crime? (Hab. 1.2–3).

And the Lord answered me and said,
  Write the vision, write it clearly on tablets
    so that it can be easily read.
For the vision must wait for its appointed hour,
  ever eager for the end, and no illusion.
If it is long in coming remain alert,
  for come it will, and not be late (Hab. 2.2–3).

Near, the supreme Day of the Lord,
  rapidly hastening on!
Bitter, the sound of the day of the Lord
  with the terrible cry of the warrior . . .
against fortified cities and proud battlements! (Zeph. 1.14–18).

Sing for joy, Maid Zion,
  exult, Israel,
be merry and glad with all your heart,
  Maid Jerusalem . . .
The Lord is there with you,
  fear no more harm . . .
Mighty to save,
  he will rejoice over you in happiness,
    making songs of his love,
      dancing with joy over you (Zeph. 3.14–17).

9

ᵍ976 973 9 70

Zephaniah, Habakkuk, Nahum –
Vision in Worship

Setting and character of Zephaniah

The heading (1.1) describes the book as the word of the Lord through Zephaniah, and indeed the focus is on the message rather than on the messenger. His family line, however, is given in unusual detail. His father's name, Cushi, means 'Ethiopian'. If his great-great-grandfather Hezekiah were the famous king, it would be understandable that an Ethiopian princess had later entered the family. Our prophet, then, may have been of royal descent, and with some Ethiopian ancestry and features. His own name meant 'Yahweh has treasured (this child)'.

The heading also locates the prophesying within the reign of Josiah (640–609). Since Zephaniah attacked Canaanite-style worship in Jerusalem (1.4), it is probable that he spoke before Josiah's great religious purge in 621, and that he was an influence leading to the reforms. We can thus date his ministry around 630.

We shall see that Jerusalem as a holy place is central in his thought, and now and again we hear the language of Zion's ceremonies (1.7; 3.5, 14–17). We may therefore envisage Zephaniah as a prophet accustomed to speak in the sphere of worship.

A century before, Amos had given the great assembly his interpretation of the Day of the Lord for which they were all longing. The prophecies of Zephaniah are arranged as a dramatic presentation of this same theme – dramatic in the sense that God's work on that tremendous day is vividly unfolded in three acts. The opening words play ominously on the Hebrew word *asiph* (referring to 'gathering away/removal') and so point to the setting of the great autumn festival for new year and Tabernacles, sometimes called 'Asiph'.

Scholars have often considered the arrangement of the prophecies to be the work of later editors, who are supposed also to have added the framework of universalist outlook and the concluding words of hope. Deeper consideration, however, reveals that all the themes belong together, and it seems wiser to ascribe them and their very significant arrangement to the original poet-prophet.

The holy centre

In Zephaniah and in other prophets and psalms we meet the view of Jerusalem as the seat of Yahweh, and so the city of central importance to the world. The idea arises from a religious experience with parallels among other ancient peoples.

In Egypt, for example, every important centre of worship claimed primacy on the grounds that it was the place where creation began. In the case of Thebes, a hymn from the fourteenth century BCE declares that she is the norm for every other city, because it was here that the earth and mankind came into being. She is as the very eye of the sun-god, the Creator, and is also called 'Opposite-her-Lord'. Every city is under her shadow, getting glory through her. (This hymn is given in Pritchard (ed), *Ancient Near Eastern Texts*, p.8.)

According to the Psalms, Jerusalem is 'the city of our God, his holy mountain, beautiful in elevation, the joy of all the earth'; Yahweh has chosen her and greatly desired her; she is his dwelling for ever; there the paradise river rises; she is mother of all peoples. (For such visionary ideals see especially Ps. 46, 48, 87 and 132.)

Zephaniah 1 – Jerusalem the centre of universal doom

In this chapter the Day of the Lord is first seen as doom for the world (two pieces, 1.2, 3), then as doom for Jerusalem in particular (four pieces, 1.4–7, 8–9, 10–11, 12–13), and finally again as doom for the world (two pieces, 1.14–16, 17–18). As in the story of the flood (Gen. 6–9), corruption is seen to pervade the whole world and to evoke the destruction of all the species along with mankind.

Zephaniah's thought is in the tradition which saw Jerusalem as a kind of 'world navel', the centre of God's communication with the world. So the prophecies easily pass from the universal doom to focus on Jerusalem and specify her offences.

First is mentioned confusion in religious loyalty. The exclusive claim of Yahweh upon his people has been swamped with customs of foreign worship. There is much worship of Baal and of star gods. Some mix their devotion, while others have turned right away from the bond with Yahweh.

Next comes condemnation of royal princes and officials. Their very clothes reflect their inclination to foreign culture, perhaps that of the Assyrian empire, within which Judah was now but a weak vassal state. They 'leap over the threshold' (1.9), in dread of in-dwelling spirits; or the sense may be that with alacrity they 'mount the podium' of the young king's throne to have his ear, yet abuse their position by using the palace for deceit and oppression.

The condemnation falls on the commercial centres of the city – the stalls in the Fish Gate, the market in the Maktesh ('hollow' or 'valley'). And as for the prosperous citizens who, whatever their nominal beliefs, in practice leave God out of the reckoning (1.12), these God will search out of their hiding places with his lamp. The prophet has compared them to wine at rest that has become thick; so they have lived at ease and become insensitive to right and compassion.

The universal perspective returns with powerful poetry that sounds the alarm as the dreadful cataclysm rushes upon the world. 'Near the supreme Day of the Lord, near and greatly hastening . . . day of trumpet and alarm, against the fortified cities and against the lofty towers!' The strong cities and castles symbolize the attempt to be secure without need of God. The Day is a fire which will rage over the whole world. If this end of an old world is preliminary to the establishment of a new, it is not said so here. The conclusion here is only that the whole world will be consumed by the fire of his 'jealousy' – his mighty will to defend and assert his right against all that would usurp it.

Zephaniah 2–3: a glimmer, then full light

The second 'act' of the drama of Yahweh's Day (2.1–3.8), like the first, is constructed with two opening pieces (2.1–2, 3–4), four central pieces (2.5–7, 8–10/11, 12, 13–15) and two concluding pieces (3.1–7, 8). But this time it is the central sections that have the world perspective, while Jerusalem is in mind in the outer sections. In the middle of the central sections, and so in the middle of the entire work, sounds a declaration of the purpose of Yahweh's warfare (2.11): he is revealing his dread holiness, so that all other powers should abandon their pretensions to grandeur; so from end to end of the world the nations will worship the true God alone.

The opening is an urgent warning to feckless people to recollect themselves before the terrible day breaks upon them (2.1–2). Then, more hopefully, there is a call to the humble and compassionate, that they should yet 'seek the Lord', 'seek what is right', 'seek humility', and so find shelter in the dreadful day (2.3).

With ominous puns, the prophet speaks of the imminent destruction of the Philistine cities near Judah's western border (2.4), and so passes into a description of the imminent divine warfare. He uses a pattern symbolic of world judgment, a pattern of four compass points, as Amos did: west (2.4/5–7), east (2.8–10), south (2.12), north (2.13–15). Then, like Amos, Zephaniah returns to the centre of judgment (3.1–8). Yes, centre of justice was Jerusalem's calling, but what a clashing contrast between the good purpose in the mind of God – that it should be the place of the Presence, the sun of compassionate rule for the world – and the actual pollution in Jerusalem's society. Princes, judges, prophets, priests, all betray their calling. So the last word here is with the all-consuming fire of judgment (3.8, cf. 1.18).

But in the third 'act' of the drama of the Day (3.9–20), the positive purpose of God's judgment emerges with fullness. The mysterious Beyond, the eternal time that will swallow up the time we now know, is indicated tersely by the two opening words, 'Then indeed'. In that wonderful time, God will give peace and love throughout society, all nations praising God and praying with pure lips. At the centre will be a truly humble and trusting people of Jerusalem. The Lord will have come to them like a lover with singing heart (3.17).

Lord of the Dance – and a question to research

With some justice the Jerusalem Bible renders Zeph. 3.17:

Yahweh your God is in your midst . . .
he will dance with shouts of joy for you
as on a day of festival.

Though the word here rendered 'dance' (*gil*) is usually rendered 'rejoice', a similar Arabic word means 'to turn round and round' and the Ethiopic equivalent means to 'dance and sing'. A much later Jewish exposition (a 'midrash') on the Song of Songs 7 states that God himself will lead the dance among the righteous in the new age. In my book *Psalms Come Alive* (p.104) I wrote:

The vision of God dancing is rich in meaning. It speaks of his dynamic nature, his relation to the physical world, his sharing in the joy of his creatures, and his commitment to the triumph of joyful love.

Zephaniah has several other rather distinctive portrayals of God. Can you pick out three?

Habakkuk: the long wait for God

The name 'Habakkuk' denotes a garden plant, perhaps 'basil'. He is emphatically designated 'the prophet' (nabi, 1.1; 3.1). All the same, his work is especially close to the forms, wording, and even musical connections of the Psalms (note the musical terms in 3.1, 9, 19). The little book also sheds valuable light on the ministry of prophets and intercessors, who were ready to link the ever-recurring themes of festal worship (God's rule as Creator, renewer of life etc) with current international crises.

The structure of the book seems to show the stages of Habakkuk's ministry in a particular crisis of the later seventh century. First we have lament, expressing to God the bad conditions of the people and so pleading for help (1.2–4). Next we have a reply which comes from God through the prophet to the people, promising relief (1.5–11). Perhaps there was for a while no sign of this relief and conditions only grew worse, for what follows is a second lament and plea to God (1.12–17). Habakkuk watched and waited (2.1) till he could bring a second reply from God (2.2–4), including words to be inscribed as a large public notice. Here, rather enigmatically, was renewed assurance and a call for patience.

Next comes a series of execrations hurled against the nation's oppressor (2.5–20). Here the prophet acts as the instrument of divine judgment and so confirms the approaching intervention of God. After a fresh heading, the last element in the book (ch. 3) unfolds as a marvellous combination of vision and intercession. As the prophet knows ever more vividly the approach of the saviour God, conqueror of Chaos, he prays for his people and finally rests in enraptured assurance.

The main clue to the date and the circumstances is in 1.6: 'Behold, I am raising up the Chaldeans.' This oracle predicts the rise of Babylonian power ('the Chaldeans') to overcome the Assyrian empire, and so can be plausibly dated a decade or so before the obvious Babylonian success of 625 onwards. Some scholars take the second lament of Habakkuk to refer to the Babylonians as having proved no better than the Assyrians. But the oppression mirrored throughout the book is most readily taken to be that perpetrated by Assyria. We can therefore see Habakkuk as continuing to lament Assyrian oppression while its hoped-for overthrow by Babylon seemed so slow in appearing.

The man in the middle

Our outline has shown the interesting structure of Habakkuk's work. A closer look now at the various sections will be rewarding, as they have much to contribute to the study of Hebrew prophecy.

Standing between God and people, he first speaks on behalf of the people (1.2–4). Here he raises complaint to God about long-standing social ills. How long must he cry and see no relief? God's rule of the world ('law', 'justice' 1.4) seems so weak and frustrated. Intercessors, we see, spoke frankly and pressed hard!

The answer comes, addressed to the (plural) people through the prophet, and still in poetry (1.5–11). The Lord here promises an amazing turn of history. With the rise of the Chaldean dynasty in Babylon, Assyria (it is implied) will reap the violence it has sown. The oracle depicts the new conquerors in anticipation with colourful ancient traditions of dreadful armies unleashed by God – hordes of horsemen, swifter than cheetahs etc. It is all quite unlike the Babylonians as they were to emerge some years later. The conclusion of the oracle (1.11) is difficult, but may be taken to summarize the purpose of this amazing and terrifying upheaval:

> At that time pride shall pass and vanish,
> and he (the Assyrian) who made his own strength his god
>   shall be brought to account.

Habakkuk now voices a second complaining prayer (1.12–17), perhaps because of delay in the relief, or simply to reinforce his first prayer and seek further confirmation in what was obviously a desperate situation. We see again the extraordinary boldness of intercessors, as they sought to sharpen their appeals. Habakkuk contrasts the almighty and righteous nature ascribed to God in traditional faith with the present wicked government of the world which God has apparently authorized. The Assyrian empire could not have arisen except through God's decree, and here it was, destroying, deporting and robbing populations at its cruel will! The subject peoples had no defender and were helpless as fish hauled up in drag-nets. (In 1.12 some of our Bibles represent the actual Hebrew text with 'we shall not die'. But originally the text will have read 'you (God) will not die' – God the All-Holy is immortal. The scribes appear to have made the alteration out of reverence.)

Having voiced his bitter 'complaint' (*tokaḥat*), Habakkuk takes up a solemn vigil, besieging God for an answer (2.1):

> I will stay at my vigil
> and station myself on siege
> and will watch to see what he will speak through me
> and what answer I must bring back concerning my
> complaint.

Like a good story-teller, he tells us this as if it is happening now, and so we are present with him in this tense moment.

Then comes God's answer, with the crucial main point held back to the end (2.2–4). First the prophet is told that the message he is to be given must be written (probably engraved on stone tablets) so that those who read it may 'run', that is, 'read it readily' (or possibly 'be encouraged'). Time will pass before the appointed hour of fulfilment, and the tablets will stand there to sustain patience and trust. The words to be written are probably just those of verse 4:

> Behold, his soul within him is puffed up, not right,
> but the righteous one shall live through his faith(fullness).

The first line refers to the oppressor, the Assyrian, suffering from the fatal disease of arrogance and so surely doomed. The second line refers to God's humble people who, through faithfully holding on to God in trust, will come through to fullness of life.

Another aspect of a prophet's work appears in the next section (2.5–20). The misconduct is described and exposed to God's judgment. Habakkuk uses rather veiled expressions – 'riddles', 'parables' (2.6), but it is not difficult to see that the pictures all relate to the Assyrian tyrant. In the prelude (2.5–6a) this great snarer of multitudes appears under the figure of 'wine' (some manuscripts have 'wealth'). Then five denunciations follow. First the tyrant is pictured as a ruthless capitalist, murderous even to the earth itself (2.6b–8). Next he is condemned as a wealthy villain who thought to live on his ill-gotten gains beyond the reach of justice (2.9–11). The third denunciation pictures the Assyrian tyrant as one who used deceit and murder to rise to power and build a city (2.12–14). This 'woe', central to the series of five, is rounded off by a fine statement of the passing of earthly empire and the victory of God's glory.

The fourth denunciation (2.15–17) pictures the oppressor as someone who abuses others in their helplessness in a drunken orgy. The key to this 'riddle' is the idea of God's judgment as a cup of overwhelming drink. The Assyrian had been an instrument of his judgment, but had then exploited the victims and would now himself have to drink and fall. His victims included the wonderful forests of Lebanon and their wild creatures, which Assyria had ruthlessly plundered. The fifth 'woe' is directed at the worshipper of idols – so the Assyrian tyrant is condemned as one devoted to false goals (2.18–19). The conclusion to the whole series announces the dreadful approach of God (2.20). The cry was probably familiar in the great temple services (cf. Zeph. 1.7; Zech. 2.13). It aptly follows the preceding threats of judgment, and also prepares for the vision of God's coming (ch. 3).

For your research

The 'woes' pronounced by Habakkuk are especially picturesque and parabolic. Can you find any other striking series of 'woes' in the Bible? And how would you explain the point and force of this rather peculiar form of denunciation? (Note that the Hebrew word rendered 'woe to' is not itself a noun, but an exclamation, 'Ah' or 'Ho!')

Music, prayer and vision

Finally, Habakkuk is filled with prophetic ecstasy as he prays for God to 'make live' the promised work of salvation (ch. 3). At the beginning and end are musical instructions ('Psalm-prayer of the prophet Habakkuk, to render in the manner of lamentations . . . Play as to seek God's favour with stringed instruments'), and the term 'Selah', common in the Psalms, occurs three times (perhaps signalling intervals for obeisance). These rubrics suggest how, after the poetry had first poured from the prophet in some great festival, it was etched in his memory and so was handed down and used as an intercessory psalm ever after (to the present day in some churches).

After the initial prayer (3.2), the visionary knowledge of God's approach grows ever stronger:

> Lord, I hear the sound of you,
> I tremble, Lord, at your work.
> In the midst of the years make it live again,
> in the midst of the years make it known again,
> in turmoil remember compassion!

> It is God, from Teman approaching,
> the Holy One, from the mountains of Paran!

From the southerly direction of the Sinai region, home of Yahweh in ancient tradition, the divine approach is sensed in the weird form of a desert storm (3.3–7); the translation should be maintained in the present tense. From 3.8 the vision takes on the colour of the storms over the sea from the north-west (these in fact often follow in reaction to the desert winds). The raging waters stand for the Chaos which the Creator subdues and turns to the service of life. In his very body the prophet has felt the force of the conflict, though it has yet to become a reality:

> I hear and my belly quakes . . .
> I groan in the day of distress
> as it rises on the host that assails us.

Then comes a kind of peace. Though the fruit of the vision is not yet grown, Habakkuk rejoices in confidence of salvation. Representative of his people and king, the prophet sings of the light-footed doe that leaps over high crags – such is the exaltation of the hope in the freedom God has prepared.

For your consideration

Habakkuk was evidently grieved at the drastic felling of the mountain-forests of the Lebanon with much destruction of wild life (2.17, cf. 2.8). Can we picture him as a sensitive man especially close to Nature, in view also of his name (expressing his mother's aspiration and influence), his gifts of intercession, poetry, music and vision, and his references to fallow-deer, horses, cheetahs (or leopards), wolves, griffon-vultures (or eagles), fish, creeping things, desert whirl-winds, raging seas, mountains, herds, figs and olives?

The character of Nahum's work

For a dozen years the vast Assyrian empire had been falling apart, when in 614 an alliance of its enemies, chiefly the Medes and Babylonians, began a series of fatal onslaughts. The capital city Nineveh, glorified by the last three great kings and dedicated to the goddess Ishtar, was captured and destroyed in 612, never to be rebuilt.

The final assault on Nineveh is the main subject of Nahum's visionary prophecy. Scenes of assault are depicted and elegies sung over the ruins. But to take the words as a real celebration after the event would be to misunderstand this kind of prophecy. Similar depictions were later given of a 'final assault' on Babylon (Isa. 46–47; Jer. 50–51); these were clearly predictions, for in the event Babylon was occupied peacefully.

Nahum rather will have spoken *before* 612 and *foretold* the end of Assyrian power, and of Nineveh in particular. After the long, long years of oppression, to which Habakkuk has borne witness, the anticipation of Assyria's end fills Nahum with exultant poetic power, and he mediates a prophecy which would be thought of as God's hammer-blow against his enemy. Like so much prophecy with vast horizons, it was probably delivered in celebration of the autumnal new year. The festival's theme of God's victorious kingship is to be realized in a great turn of history (cf. 1.15 in conjunction with Isa. 52.7).

Nahum is sometimes blamed as a 'nationalist' prophet. He sees the foe as God's foe, and has no denunciation for his own people. But his fault is to have dealt with only one aspect of the imminent turn of events – the good news of the oppressor's end. His ministry may have been broader, but it was this contribution which was preserved. He was remembered in accordance with his name 'Nahum': '(God is) comforting'.

The utterances fall into two cycles, covering the same ground with difference of emphasis, each confirming the other: 1.2–2.12 and 2.13–3.19. Each shows how Yahweh challenges his enemy, launches his attack and is victorious, and each ends with a dirge over the fallen foe.

The force of Nahum's poem

At the outset, Nahum sees and depicts the advance of God against the evil power that would usurp his kingdom. The 'jealous' and 'vengeful' aspect of Yahweh means that he is passionately determined to right the wrongs and save the poor and oppressed. His martial 'fury' signals his power to break the presumptuous tyranny. Through the opening of the prophet's poem flow traditional phrases. He draws on a hymn which used successive letters of the alphabet to begin its lines. The ancient theme of power against seas and mountains speaks of the Creator's 'battle' that turns Chaos into a beautiful order.

As the prophet gave expression to his vision, his voice and gestures will have made clear who is addressed in 1.9–15 (where Hebrew distinguishes masculines and feminines, singulars and plurals in the occurrences of 'you' and 'your'). It is a dramatic scene, where the opponents of the Lord are indeed the Assyrians, Nineveh and their leaders, but at a deeper level are the Assyrian deities and the rebellious forces of Chaos. Words of hope are spoken to the oppressed peoples, especially Judah. The 'good tidings' of God's triumphant kingdom, regularly proclaimed in the midst of the annual festivals, will take on political reality as Assyria meets her doom (1.15).

The vision now concentrates on the storming of the enemy city. Nineveh is not named till 2.8, and the attacking armies still have a supernatural quality, blazing with light and fire. Every bastion is quickly stormed, and a mighty flood is unleashed against Ishtar's temple. Ishtar's image is led off into captivity. The death of the tyrant city is emphasized by the chanting of her funeral dirge, which pictures her as a lion's den where much prey has been devoured (2.11–12).

The bravery of King Josiah

Babylonian tablets in the British Museum give a chronicle of the last years of the Assyrian empire. After Nineveh had been taken by the Medes and Babylonians in 612, the Assyrian king and his army retreated northwards. Here they were finally crushed in the battle of Haran in 609.

A great Egyptian army had not arrived in time to save them. Pharaoh Necho had hoped to support the remnant of Assyria and so thwart the menace of the rising power of Babylon. What had so fatefully delayed him?

The great fortress of Megiddo, in the passes of Mount Carmel, lay in his path. Here his way was blocked by the last great Judean king, Josiah. At the cost of his life (II Kings 23.29), Josiah seems to have succeeded in sealing the fate of the Assyrian power which had so long oppressed his people.

As though to add weight and confirmation to the foregoing presentation of Assyria's doom, the poem now portrays it all a second time (2.13–3.19). Again the advance of God to challenge his foe is envisaged. Again the word of judgment is pronounced and the downfall of Nineveh foreseen. And again a concluding ironic lament (3.18–19) celebrates the end of the cruel empire.

This second cycle is no less brilliant and passionate than the first. The speed and the din of the assault are portrayed in vivid staccato phrases. The 'bloody city' is pictured as a destructive arch-harlot, at last pilloried and publicly shamed. This reflects the cult of Nineveh's chief deity, Ishtar, who was a fertility goddess attended by sacred harlots, and sometimes pictured even by her worshippers as a killer.

The Egyptian capital Thebes, despite its strong position by the Nile, had been sacked by the Assyrians in 663 (3.8). No less would mighty Nineveh fall an easy prey. The voracious officials of the Assyrian empire (armies of occupation, political agents and inspectors, exactors of tribute and tax) will vanish as locust swarms in their time take wing and disappear over the horizon. Generals and governors sleep the sleep of death. The end of the Assyrian king is marked, not with mourning, but with universal applause.

So Nahum sees and declares his vision of God's forthcoming action against the greatest worldly power ever known. His poetry is vibrant with power, and for Nahum this is the power of God already going forth to effect salvation. Eventually he wrote it all down, a still potent record. When Nineveh was destroyed in 612, the vision was confirmed and so judged worthy of preservation for all time.

For discussion or writing

– Nahum has been described as the most brilliant of Hebrew poets. Making allowance for the inevitable loss of poetic power in translation, can you collect evidence for his brilliance?

– Zephaniah, Habakkuk and Nahum worked in Judah and were fairly close in date. Summarize what their ministries had in common, and what was distinctive in each.

THE VOICE OF JEREMIAH

Be horrified, heavens, at this,
    shudder, be greatly shocked, says the Lord.
Two wrongs my people have done:
    me they have forsaken, their well of living water,
    to hew for themselves cisterns,
        cracked cisterns that cannot hold water
                            (2.12–13).

I see the earth – look, it dissolves into chaos.
    I see the heavens – their light is gone.
I see the mountains, and look, they quake
    and all the heights are reeling.
I see, and look, no people are left
    and all the birds have fled (4.24–25).

The prophets they prophesy lies;
    the priests, they follow the directions of the prophets.
And my people, that is how they like it (5.31).

Even the stork in the sky knows her right times,
    and turtle-dove, swallow and crane
    keep their proper time for returning.
But my people do not know the Lord's rule for them
                            (8.7).

Oh that my head were waters
    and my eyes a well of tears,
that I might weep day and night
    for the slain of my poor people! (9.1).

The people that escaped the sword
    found grace in the wilderness . . .
With an everlasting love I love you
    And so I willl keep faith wih you for ever (31.2–3).

10

Jeremiah – The Cost of Prophecy

We find three main kinds of material in the book: (a) vivid and emotional poetic prophecy (e.g. 2.2b–3); (b) biography – stories related by another about Jeremiah, rather precise and factual, sometimes providing a framework for a prose discourse by the prophet (e.g. much of chapters 34–45); (c) discourses in a repetitive style like that of Deuteronomy, often introduced as the Lord's word that came 'to Jeremiah' or 'to me' (e.g. 11.1–17).

Of these kinds the first will bring us Jeremiah's own voice most directly, the second seems to have come from well-informed companions like Baruch (36.4; 43.3; 45.1–5), while the third is based on good tradition but develops the speech at length for the warning of a later generation. The three kinds represent three streams of tradition about Jeremiah which were worked together through several stages and editions to reach the present form.

Jeremiah's early ministry

The last mighty king of the Assyrian empire, Ashurbanipal, died about the year of Jeremiah's call (627). So hints of change in the world order may have played a part in opening Jeremiah's heart to the divine message.

The name 'Jeremiah' may have been given as a prayer in a time of sorrow – 'May the Lord raise up'. His family were from a priesthood rooted outside Jerusalem, tracing their ancestry to the priests of old Israel (1.1, cf. I Kings 2.26–27). Accordingly, he was to agonize, not only for the inhabitants of Judah, but also for the clans to the north (Ephraim, Benjamim etc).

In Jerusalem the child-king Josiah was coming of age, and religious reform was in the air. Jeremiah's early preaching (chs. 2–6) denounces the worship of Baal and the oppression of the poor. He foretells judgment in the form of invaders from the north (the main line of access) and he trembles with alarm as he senses the future havoc. There are many impressive passages in the materials relating to this period.

His call (ch. 1) is reported with stress on God's purpose for him. Even before God had completed his fashioning in the womb, he 'knew' him (chose him for a great mission), claimed him, and appointed him nabi over the nations. The phrases here have a ring of royal language, for Jeremiah is to represent and speak mightily for God. But the man himself is shy, sensitive and self-doubting, quick to excuse himself from the great responsibility. Only from God could he find the necessary strength. The experience is more direct and personal than that of other prophets. He sees the Lord himself stretch out his hand, touch his mouth, and put into his mouth words with the power to break down or rebuild kingdoms.

The things of everyday life are now full of deeper meaning. Poet and prophet, he sees with the heart. The flowering almond tree (Hebrew *shaqed*) tells him of the One who is awake (Hebrew *shoqed*) and watchful to fulfil his word. The boiling cauldron, perhaps with steam, smoke and flames blown from the north, tells him of cities in flames, streams of refugees, conquerors advancing on Jerusalem from the north, instruments of divine judgment.

His early preaching is vivid with imagery. Israel in the desert days was a young bride devotedly following her husband; she was the Lord's, and his alone, holy to him as the consecrated first-fruits of harvest (2.1–3). But later she sought other gods, restless in her desire as a camel or a wild ass on heat (2.23–24). This is a people who would forsake a spring of living water, preferring to make for themselves cisterns where water would grow stale and leak away (2.12–13). The skies are appalled to witness it.

Yes, skies, land, and indeed all creatures must suffer from the people's lust for false goals. True poet, true prophet, Jeremiah sees through to the end of the matter. A silent, wasted earth surrounds him – darkened skies, trembling hills, empty of people, empty of birds, in the day of the final reckoning (4.23–26).

A note of urgency and alarm sounds especially in chapter 5. He hears the Lord's urgent order to his angels to run up and down the streets of Jerusalem 'to see if you can find anyone acting fairly and faithfully, so that I can forgive (the city)'. The prophet wonders if it is only the poor and ignorant who do not know the Lord's requirements; surely the educated, well-off classes know better! But alas, he finds these too have all scorned the Lord's wishes. They have 'broken the yoke' and 'snapped the traces'. And the worst of it is that there is a chain of collusion. The prophets prophesy falsehood, the priests accept their direction, and the ordinary people like it that way.

In Israelite society it was extremely rare for men not to marry. Jeremiah's sense of loneliness was intensified by his conviction that he must remain single. It was to be a sign of the terrible threat that hung over society (16.1–4).

Years of national reform

A second phase of ministry can be found in the exciting years that followed the discovery of the awe-inspiring document in the temple in 621 (II Kings 22). King Josiah, till his death in 609, acted vigorously in accordance with this document (probably connected with our Deuteronomy) which set out the terms of Yahweh's covenant with Israel. Heeding these commands of Yahweh, Josiah purged the worship, centred it on Jerusalem and destroyed other sanctuaries.

Jeremiah's role in this period is not well evidenced. He may have preached in favour of the reforming covenant (Jer. 11.1–17) and risked death for it (11.18–23). Some think he came to criticize reforming scribes (8.8–9). Some suggest that prophecies of revival for the northern clans (30.15–20 etc) may be rooted in this period, when Josiah was able to gather back some of their territories into his kingdom.

For your consideration

Is it plausible that Jeremiah, young and sensitive, may
have first supported the reformers, and later attacked
them as false scribes? Do you think 8.8–9 can best be
explained along these lines?

Jerusalem heads for destruction

Most of the stories of Jeremiah's ministry belong to a third phase,
from the death of King Josiah in 609 to the destruction of
Jerusalem in 587. The main reigns were those of Josiah's sons
Jehoiaqim (609–598) and Zedekiah (597–587). The former was
tyrannical and hostile to Jeremiah. The latter was well disposed,
but unable to control the final slide of the kingdom into disaster.

Jehoiaqim was a vassal of the Babylonians, the new world-
power. Jeremiah counselled loyalty to this arrangement, but in
vain. When circumstances beckoned, Jehoiaqim tried to throw
off his allegiance. And so there came the first Babylonian assault
on Jerusalem, and a great deportation of royalty (including the
recently crowned young Jehoiachin), priests and skilled classes
(in 597).

Jeremiah remained to suffer in Jerusalem for another decade,
till the armies came again to crush another rebellion. Scenes like
those of Jeremiah 38 (the prophet thrown into a deep and miry
cistern) belong to the years when the city was under siege. In 587
(some give the date as 586) city and temple were destroyed, many
were put to death, and others taken into exile.

Looking at this period in more detail, we note that Jeremiah
narrowly escaped execution at the outset of Jehoiaqim's reign for
prophesying against the holy city and its temple (chs. 7 and 26).
The address he delivered in the temple gate was not scornful of
the sanctity of the temple. On the contrary, it was because of the
special presence of God in his 'house', through his 'name', that

hypocritical worship must cause an explosion – 'Will you steal, murder, commit adultery . . . and go after other gods . . . and then come and stand before me in this house which is called by my name, and say "We are delivered"?' Again and again, at every crisis for national policy, the people of Jerusalem re-assured themselves from the fact that the temple of the Lord lay within the walls, but where was the safety when they violated the holy place, making it a den of robbers?

Jehoiaqim set about building himself a fine palace, and earned Jeremiah's condemnation (22.13–19): 'Do you think you are a king because you compete in cedar?' The grandiose plans were financed by injustice. What a contrast with the previous king, Josiah, who had protected the poor! 'Was not this to know me? says the Lord.'

Perhaps it was about this time that Jeremiah watched a potter at work and listened for Yahweh's word (18.1–11). Sometimes the clay would not shape in the potter's hand as he intended, the clay being of variable quality. He would then press it together and make it into another kind of vessel, as seemed best to him. Jeremiah saw here a parable of God's work with his people. In sovereign power he is ready to deal with them in judgment or mercy, as seems best to him.

Dated to the fourth year of Jehoiaqim (606/5) is the incident of the dictated prophecies related in chapter 36. For over twenty years Jeremiah had been speaking prophecies, which he had retained in a sequence in his memory, no doubt the normal prophetic custom. Now he dictated them to an assistant, the scribe Baruch, who wrote them on a scroll and read them out publicly in the temple on the occasion of a day of fasting and penitence. The whole procedure may have been resorted to because Jeremiah at that time was not allowed to go to the temple. But perhaps there was also the hope that the scroll would make an overwhelming impression, confronting the king and people with the objective and continuing threat of Yahweh's words. It was a prophetic sign, an act of power.

Jehoiaqim rose to the challenge. As each part was read to him, he solemnly cut it off with a knife and burnt it in a brazier. So he signified that the threat was nullified. He was unable, however, to arrest Jeremiah and Baruch, who had already gone into hiding on the advice of friendly officials. While in hiding, the story concludes, Jeremiah dictated the scroll afresh to Baruch with appropriate additions, thus renewing the sign of powerful warning. Here then was a circumstance where the oracles were more safely preserved in the memory than in writing, but where memory and writing each had a part to play.

In Zedekiah's reign, following the surrender and deportations of 597, Jeremiah's sufferings arose from his opposition to a fresh rebellion against Babylon. He declared the Babylonian monarch Nebuchadnezzar to be Yahweh's Servant. He symbolized the divinely appointed yoke of Babylon by wearing a yoke, and when a nationalist prophet solemnly broke it, he replaced it with a yoke of iron (chs. 27–28). He sent a letter containing an oracle to the exiles, predicting a long stay and urging them to pray for the welfare of Babylon (ch. 29). And he stressed their value in God's eyes; compared with the new leaders in Jerusalem, they were the 'good figs' (ch. 24).

The leaders in Jerusalem could not resist attempting a new rebellion, and so the Babylonians came again and laid siege to the city. Now Jeremiah's situation was acutely dangerous. He suffered the ultimate imprisonment when he was lowered into a cistern, a deep cylinder cut into the rock under the city to store water, and holding only cold mire in its dreadful darkness. But help came when an Ethiopian official in the palace obtained Zedekiah's permission to rescue the prophet, and with a party of men carefully drew the emaciated sufferer on ropes and rags up to safety (38.1–13).

Jeremiah was still kept under guard, as the situation of the encircled city grew worse. In this dark hour he was moved to perform a symbolic action which promised that the land would one day return to normal life, since nothing was too hard for the Lord. A relation of Jeremiah's was trying to raise money by selling a field in Anathoth, and Jeremiah had the right and duty to redeem it and keep it in the family. Conscious of Yahweh's work in it all, he weighed out the silver and had the transaction carefully recorded for posterity as the law required. One scroll was bound and sealed against tampering, and a copy left as an open scroll for convenient reference; then both scrolls were placed for safe keeping in a long earthenware jar. The message of hope was not expressed in extravagant language, but yet in that situation was wonderful: 'Houses and fields and vineyards shall again be bought in this land.'

A creative task

The incidents just surveyed could lend themselves to the making of a short play about Jeremiah and the siege of Jerusalem. Can you make an outline sketch of such a play, suggest a title, and compose a psalm-prayer that Jeremiah might have uttered in the cistern, drawing on Ps. 69.1–4 and 40.1–3?

With the short-lived government in Mispah

Having destroyed Jerusalem in 587, blinded and chained Zedekiah, and deported him with many others, the Babylonians set up a new administration eight miles to the north at Mispah. The governor, Gedaliah, had Jeremiah to counsel him, for the Babylonians had identified the prophet, released him from a column of captives and given him the option to remain (40.1–6). Remnants of the army also came in from the wilds to join them, and the new beginning seemed blessed in the good fruit-harvest (40.7–12).

Some of Jeremiah's hopeful prophecies may have originated in this situation, or have been resumed then from the hopeful days of King Josiah. Jeremiah, the most sensitive of prophets, had heard the ancestral mother weeping and wailing as her children were driven away into exile, and in the mystery of God's time-transcending purposes he had promised her their return

---

In the world of Jeremiah

Here are three small but striking examples of archaeological discoveries which put us in the very steps of Jeremiah. From Lachish comes a clay seal-impression from a document sent by Gedaliah when he was the king's chief minister; it reads, 'Of Gedaliah who is Over-the-House'. From Mispah (Tell en-Nasbeh) comes the actual seal of Jaazaniah, one of the commanders who was there with Jeremiah (40.8); it has the emblem of a fighting cock and the words 'Of Jaazaniah, servant of the king'. And it seems likely that a more recently discovered seal-impression ('Of Brkyahu, son of Neriyahu, the scribe') is that of Jeremiah's friend Baruch!

(31.15–17). He now reaffirmed this wonderful restoration, a time of praise on the holy mountain, abundance in Nature, souls refreshed like a watered garden, a time to dance (31.10–14). A new covenant with God would replace the broken bonds of the past (31.31–34, discussed below).

This good interlude may have lasted five years, or much less. Gedaliah and the Babylonian garrison were treacherously murdered by one of the Davidic family (ch. 41). The survivors of the government fled to Egypt, taking with them an unwilling Jeremiah (chs. 42–43).

For your consideration

Can you find any recurring characteristics in the hopeful prophecies of ch. 31?

Jeremiah's end in Egypt

The fugitives followed the coastal route and entered the Nile Delta region at the city of Tahpanhes (Daphne, Tell Defneh). In front of the main government building Jeremiah prophesied with a symbolic action. The stones that he buried were, he said, to be one day a foundation for Nebuchadnezzar's throne when he came 'to clean the land of Egypt as a shepherd cleans his cloak of lice' (43.8–13). A fragmentary record may indicate that Nebuchadnezzar did actually campaign briefly in Egypt in 568.

There were substantial Jewish settlements in Egypt. Some of them had a religion like that attacked by Josiah's reforms. The women in particular offered devotion to the great Semitic fertility goddess, 'the queen of heaven'. The last glimpse of Jeremiah shows him in dispute with them. They say, with some logic, that the nation has had nothing but disaster since Josiah prohibited the 'fertility' worship. Jeremiah replies with a word of judgment from Yahweh, concluding, 'They shall know whose word shall stand, mine or theirs' (ch. 44).

Jeremiah's end is not recorded in the Bible, but a later legend recounted that he was stoned to death by the settlers.

One soul – and the fate of a nation

We have seen that there is an unusual abundance of material about the outer circumstances and events in Jeremiah's life. But in addition we have a series of passages which seem to offer an unparalleled insight into the prophet's inner spiritual struggles.

Some indeed have traced in these passages a religious revolution. 'It was a great step in the history of religion' wrote J. Skinner (*Prophecy and Religion*, p.227) 'to turn from the formalism of an external worship, and the legalism of a national covenant, to find God in the heart of an individual . . . Jeremiah took that step, and opened up a way of access to God which many devout souls, following in his footprints, found to be the way everlasting.'

Further study, however, has shown that Jeremiah in these passages was using patterns of thought and phraseology which already had a long history. The lamenting psalms did not take their rise from Jeremiah, as Skinner thought, but were rooted in ancient, and indeed international, worship.

Over-reacting to this discovery, some scholars now saw

Jeremiah as voicing here only his community's anguish; he was their spokesman, using traditional forms of prayer. Some even went further and inclined to see these passages as composed for the community after Jeremiah's time.

A more balanced view should begin by recognizing that Jeremiah, with his background in the priesthood and his calling to be a wholly dedicated nabi, will have been skilled in the ancient style of intercession. He will often have led public prayer with words and thoughts like those of the ancient lamenting psalms, and he will sometimes have been able, like Habakkuk, to bring back God's answers to the people, again in traditional style.

The time came when he had a heavy problem to pray about, heavy with consequence both for the community and for him personally. The problem was to know whether or not he was deceived in his message for the nation, for there were many prophets who opposed him. Would God vindicate him and shame his adversaries? On the answer hung the fate of Jeremiah personally and also the fate of the holy city and people.

So he prayed and listened for answers in the traditional way, which did not prevent him from expressing his own passion and anguished circumstances. He will have prayed thus repeatedly, with intense concentration, and so would remember exactly what he had chanted and what oracles came to him in reply. He will have passed on the memory of these transactions as solemnly as he did his other inspirations. His close associates preserved them as part of that precious legacy of prophecy, which more and more shed light on the upheavals that befell the nation.

These dialogues with God, the so-called Confessions of Jeremiah, may be outlined as follows. In the first (11.18–23) he tells of a revelation that has come to him about about a plot to kill him. He appeals to the Lord to bring retribution on the plotters. He receives the answer that God will deal with the adversaries, who are men of Jeremiah's village, Anathoth, and who have told him not to prophesy.

The second passage (12.1–6) addresses God with sharp complaint: celebrated as righteous, God yet plants the wicked and lets them take root! But Jeremiah fights on with his weapon

---

A sample of St Augustine's Confessions (X.6)

This is the fruit of my confessions of what I am, not of what I have been: to confess this, not before thee only, in a secret exultation with trembling and a secret sorrow with hope, but in the ears also of the believing sons of men, sharers of my joy and partners in my mortality, my fellow citizens and fellow pilgrims, who are gone before or are to follow on, companions of my way. These are thy servants, my brethren, whom thou willest to be thy sons; my masters whom thou commandest me to serve, if I would live with thee, of thee . . . This then I do in deed and word, this I do under thy wings; in over great peril, were not my soul subdued unto thee under thy wings, and my infirmity known unto thee. I am a little one, but my Father ever liveth, and my Guardian is sufficient for me. For he is the same who begat me and defends me, and thou thyself art all my good, thou Almighty, who art with me, yea, before I am with thee.

---

of prayer: 'Pull them out like sheep for the slaughter!' The answer he receives only tells him to prepare for worse; even his brothers may betray him.

In the third passage (15.10–11, 15–21) Jeremiah laments that he is a cause of strife, hated it seems by all, though he has interceded for the nation's safety. In his devotion to God's word he has had to sit alone – 'Oh why is my pain unceasing, my wound incurable? Will you be to me like a deceitful brook, like waters that fail?' He receives the answer that if he returns to God afresh, utters only what is precious, and not what is worthless, he will be like the mouth of God and overcome his enemies. The allusion to 'what is worthless' may respond to the bitter words of Jeremiah's prayer. Otherwise it may be an indication of the unworthiness and need for cleansing which Jeremiah feels in his drawing near to God.

The fourth passage (17.14–18) finds the prophet praying for healing and salvation. He laments the mocking of adversaries, protests his innocence of wishing evil on his people, expresses trust in the Lord's protection, and prays for destruction upon his persecutors. All these thoughts are regular motifs in the ancient psalms of lament.

For the fifth passage (18.18–23) the scene is set by a preliminary verse in prose (18.18). The adversaries are incensed at Jeremiah's condemnation of the city's moral leadership (priests, sages and prophets) and resolve to strike him down 'with the tongue', that is with a curse or through accusations. Jeremiah's prayer begins with a plea for a hearing and then argues that his enemies are returning evil for good. In terms like those of the most lurid psalms (e.g. 109), he asks for death to fall on the enemies and all their families. It is as though he were summoning up the most fearsome imprecations to counter the words with which his enemies were planning to strike him down.

The sixth passage (20.7–18) finds Jeremiah putting it to God that he has deceived or tricked him. He seems to be haunted by the fear that God, for some inscrutable purpose, has filled him with a false message, resulting only in a general response of mockery and hate. He feels that God in his power has put him in this position with no way of escape. If he tries to repress the message God has given him, it scorches the bones within him, and becomes a blazing fire in his heart, till he must give way and speak it. The traditional pattern of lamenting prayer leads him to express confidence that God will help him, and even to begin the song of praise for deliverance. But it is to no avail. There is no signal of help. The dark closes in again. So the conclusion shows Jeremiah uttering a solemn curse on the day that saw his birth, and on the good person who, expecting a blessing, ran with the news to his father. Better had the man killed him while still in the womb!

Jeremiah has reached here the extremes of lamenting prayer. God can no longer be addressed, nor his name mentioned. Only the terrible wish can be uttered, the wish that he had never existed. It is a cry from the bottom of the pit – yet still a cry, the hope of moving the Lord not quite extinguished. The book shows that ghost of a hope as not in vain, for Jeremiah's ministry and life were to continue for many years, years of courage and faithfulness.

A new covenant – written on the heart!

The little prophecy of a new covenant (31.31–34) was, according to J.Skinner (*Prophecy and Religion*, p.332), Jeremiah's most noteworthy contribution to the ideal religion of the future. But some have disparaged it as written in prose, echoing thoughts and words of Deuteronomy, and lacking the themes of repentance and hope for the nations. It is hardly, they say, the work of an original and penetrating poet like Jeremiah.

An old-style appreciation

A warm tribute to Jeremiah was written by G.G. Findlay in Hastings' *Dictionary of the Bible* (revised by J.Mauchline in the 1963 edition). Here is an extract:

Jeremiah's poetry is unrivalled in the records of Semitic antiquity in the intensity of its lyricism, its dramatic power, its abundance of memorable images, its sensuousness and passionateness, its immediacy of response to every mood of nature and every nuance of the soul of man. His intimate self-disclosure in the so-called 'Confessions' exposes to us the very depths of his soul; only in Job and the Apostle Paul and Augustine and Luther and Kierkegaard do we encounter anything similar.

He is a Hebrew Wordsworth in his feeling for the hidden mystery within the world of created things . . . But while he could observe the blossoming almond in the early spring (1.11–12), the hot air of the sirocco (4.11), the migratory impulse within the stork and the times of the turtle-dove, swallow and crane (8.4), the inchoate drive of the young camel and the sexual urge of the wild ass (2.23–24), and even the pathos of the heavens and earth (2.13; 4.23–26), they were for him but sign and symbol of Yahweh's active sovereignty.

In so short an oracle, however, it is hardly surprising that some themes of salvation are not treated. The emphasis falls on what God does, when all human effort has failed. The oracle aims to announce one tremendous thing, a work of sheer grace at the heart of his creation, and it does so most effectively. As regards resemblance to Deuteronomy, it is likely that Jeremiah and his associates were close to the scribal circles in question, and in prose would use a similar style. Prose would seem appropriate for a description of a covenant. The passage still arises from vision and faith, and is worthy of a great prophet's insights.

Balm of Gilead

Some of the most brilliant poetry in the Book of Jeremiah occurs in the oracles concerning foreign nations collected in chs. 46–51. In the Greek translation (from about the third century BCE) these oracles are in a different order and the whole is placed after 25.13. Another fact to reckon with is that some of the material in these passages closely resembles or even duplicates oracles found in other prophetic books.

This material seems to have come from the traditions of prophetic circles of the seventh and sixth centuries and may not have been especially connected with Jeremiah's prophesying. The first two oracles, concerning the fateful clash between Babylon and Egypt in 605, are the easiest to ascribe to him (46.3–12; 46.14–24). The Babylonian victory is predicted; the wounds of Egypt will not be readily healed, not even by the famed aromatic balm from the forests of Gilead, east of the Jordan. As it turned out, the Egyptian army was annihilated at the battle of Carchemish (605).

Other oracles concern the Philistines, Moab, Ammon, Edom, some Arab tribes, Elam, and the fate of Babylon (which in the event turned out quite differently). It is a kind of prophesying like that we have met in Nahum.

The promise has the form of an oracle, where the Lord speaks in the first person. The time is coming, he says, when he will make a new covenant with Israel and Judah. It will still embody a close relationship, like a marriage bond, between God and people, but whereas the old covenant was broken through human unfaithfulness, the new one will endure because of God's marvellous action. He will write his requirements on their heart, so that in their deepest being they will be responsive to his will. And the estrangement made by former sins will have been swept away through his work of forgiveness. A sign of the marvel will be that religious teaching will be unnecessary, for all of themselves will know him – living in true fellowship and communion with him.

Here indeed the vision leaps beyond the realities of history into the ultimate. Many centuries and revelations later, there is no sign that the teachers of faith and morals are not needed. But the promise finds a beginning of fulfilment wherever there is experience of a decisive new approach from God, of a profound change of hearts, of forgiveness, and of a resultant life of communion.

For discussion or writing

– If you were asked to prepare a plan or outline-script for a half-hour programme on Jeremiah (e.g. for BBC Radio 4), how would you set about it? Can you complete such a plan?

– Imagine Baruch kept a diary of private comments during his time with Jeremiah, and some parts have come to light. Can you provide some extracts?

– The phrase 'the New Testament' arises from the Hebrew for the 'new covenant'. To what extent is it an appropriate name for the Christian scripture, in view of its first use in Jer. 31.31?

THE VOICE OF EZEKIEL

In the thirtieth year, in the fourth month, on the fifth day,
as I was in the midst of the exiled people by the Great Canal,
the heavens opened and I saw visions of God (1.1).

And on the dais above the heads of the angelic steeds
was the likeness of a sapphire in the form of a throne,
and on the form of a throne was a form like a man's . . .

Like the appearance of the bow in the clouds on a day of rain,
such was the appearance of the brightness all around.
This was the appearance of the form of the Glory of the Lord,
and I saw and fell upon my face (1.26, 28).

What is this proverb that you have about the land of Israel –
'The days grow long and every vision comes to nothing'? . . .
I will put an end to this proverb . . .
I the Lord will speak the word that I will speak,
and it will be done and no more delayed (12.21–25).

Thus says the Lord Yahweh,
See, it is I, I myself,
who will search for my sheep and seek them out . . .
I will seek the lost and bring back those driven away,
and I will bandage the injured and strengthen the weak,
and keep watch over the strong and healthy,
as a good shepherd to them (34.11, 16).

And I will sprinkle clean water over you
and you will be cleansed of all that defiles you,
and I will clean you from all your idols
and give you a new heart
and put a new spirit within you.
I will remove from your bodies the heart of stone
and give you a heart warm and living (36.25–26).

11

Ezekiel – A Priest Swept
by the Spirit

A rich and peculiar book

The large book bearing Ezekiel's name is well-ordered. It can be divided into six sections:

(1) the extraordinary account of his call to ministry (chs. 1–3)
(2) his predictions of Jerusalem's doom (4–24)
(3) his oracles against other nations such as Tyre and Egypt (25–32)
(4) his message of hope following Jerusalem's destruction (33–37)
(5) predictions of strange battles and upheavals (the mysterious Gog and Magog, 38–39)
(6) a long and detailed vision of a new society around a new holy centre (40–48)

The style of the book is distinctive. From the old priesthood comes the love of formulas (a favourite phrase may recur nearly a hundred times!) and the heavy lawyer-like precision. From the charismatic prophet comes the powerful imagery with its mighty messages. These priestly and charismatic elements are fused together in the book, as they were no doubt also in the personality of Ezekiel.

One cannot, however, determine exactly where Ezekiel's authorship ends and the expansions of his followers begin. It seems likely that, while the bulk of the material comes from the great priest-prophet, editing and expanding was done in a circle close to him (perhaps the priestly clan called 'Ezekiel'/'Yehezqel', one of twenty-four duty-groups – in Hebrew the name in 1.3 and I Chron. 24.16 is spelt the same).

The life of a priest turned prophet and pastor

In 597, as we have noted in connection with Jeremiah, the Babylonians subdued a rebellion by deporting the youth-king Jehoiachin, other royalty, priests, professionals and artisans to Babylonia, where most were given settlements in ordered communities. Jehoiachin's young uncle, Zedekiah, was installed in his place as king in Jerusalem, and Judah had a last chance to live with loyal submission in the Babylonian empire.

Ezekiel the priest will have been among the deported people. After a few years, in 593, he experienced a great revelation of God and a call to be his prophet (1.1–3). The exiled people now looked to him for guidance about the prospects of Jerusalem and for themselves. Repeatedly he answered that he foresaw a final disaster. He was formally consulted by the elders (8.1) and compared himself to a watchman guarding the people's life (3.16–21) or a wall shielding them from divine assault (13.1–5).

When news came of another rebellion crushed and Jerusalem in ruins (587), he began to tell of God's purpose for restoration. He launched some of the greatest images of hope and resurrected life. The latest date reflected in the book is 571, the raising of the siege of Tyre (29.18). So it is probable that he died well before the Exile came to an end in 539.

Ezekiel often felt called to enact or to be a 'sign' (Hebrew *mopheth, oth*, 4.3; 12.6, 11 etc) and this idea seems to sum up the meaning of his ministry. So drastically taken into the service of the Lord, his life was significant now only in pointing to the mysterious working of God and, at a deeper level, in making that work present. He was called to embody the word of God.

Just before the destruction of Jerusalem in 587, Ezekiel knew that his beloved wife was about to die (24.15). The personal tragedy became a sign in the tragedy of the beloved Jerusalem. He surprised the people by not carrying out the mourning customs when his wife died. He did not remove his turban, cover his lip or eat mourner's bread. He explained that his conduct was a word of God: *they* were about to lose the delight of their eyes, the holy city, and they would be too appalled to carry out rites of mourning.

Ezekiel was deeply and painfully engaged in many symbolic actions as part of his prophesying. We find him making representations of Jerusalem under siege, and with long vigils signifying the perseverence of the besiegers (4.1–3). He lies bound on the earth for many days, bearing Israel's sin and punishment, in sign of many years of exile to come (4.4–8). We find him acting out a famine (4.9–17) and the various fates of conquered citizens (5.1–4).

Only too clear was the meaning when he made a bundle of his belongings, as he and his companions had done for their march into exile ten years before. At dusk he broke a hole through the wall of his house and crawled out, shouldered his bundle and set off into the darkness. In all this the assembled onlookers saw the fate of those who till now had remained in Jerusalem. Through the ruined walls they would troop with their pathetic burdens and tread the endless stony way to exile (12.1–11).

In all these dramatic signs Ezekiel gave himself to powerful expressions of Yahweh's word. He believed that the Lord was at work in the signs, shaping events and declaring their meaning. The prophet's role was to be the faithful and obedient instrument.

Ezekiel's location

Ezekiel's involvement with the destiny of Jerusalem between 597 and 587 is so vivid that some scholars have supposed that he must have been physically in the city (see for example 11.13). But attempts to replot his life-course inevitably became very speculative, and it is best to follow the indications carefully given in the book.

The chariot of God

Priestly experience of God was bound up with the sanctuary and its routines, special places, times and rites. The uprooting of priests and leading people from Jerusalem, along with the display of power by foreign armies and their gods, could therefore have spelt religious confusion and dismay for Ezekiel the priest and his companions. So the great vision of Yahweh described in chapters 1–3 was of decisive importance, both for Ezekiel's life and for the continuance of Israel's faith.

In religious imagery common in the ancient world, a message came of Yahweh's continuing governance of the universe and of Israel, his freedom to be present in glory wherever he willed, and his immediate purposes to be worked out through his exiled servants. In that situation it was a mighty message. Yet it was more than a message, for through his report of his vision, Ezekiel was sharing his experience of the reality of the Highest, God who had come nigh, taken from him all his strength, and breathed new life into him through the Spirit. Of all that the vision meant, Ezekiel was henceforth the living sign and servant.

A mighty symbol and a task of research

Yahweh's 'Spirit' (Hebrew *ruah*) is prominent in the experience of Ezekiel. The word *ruah* (usually feminine) can mean 'wind', 'breath', and 'spirit', and often something of all three. It provided a rich and evocative image of the creative power of God, a force going out to effect his will, but also bringing experience of his very being and presence. Here are some examples of usage which are fruitful to consider: Gen. 1.2; Ps. 104.29–30; Ezek. 37.1, 5, 8, 9, 10, 14, 22; Judg. 6.34; Isa. 11.2; 63.9–10; Hag. 2.5; Ps. 51.10–11. What are the main threads that you notice here?

It happened by the main canal near Babylon, perhaps in a place where the exiles met for worship (cf. Ps.137.1). In his trance Ezekiel saw the vault that undergirded the heavens torn open, and the chariot of God coming through and driving right up to him. Appearing first as a ball of cloud and fire, it emerged at closer range as a vehicle drawn by sphinx-like beings. It was marvellously mobile, all directions being open to it. On a crystal-clear dais in the chariot was a blue throne in a circle of rainbow-light, and in the circle was a man-like figure – the form of the manifestation of Yahweh, Creator and Lord.

For Ezekiel it was a stupendous experience, which inaugurated an arduous ministry and a life of absorption with the divine will and word.

Dialogue with the people – repent and live!

Ezekiel lived in the midst of the compact community of exiles, and many of his sayings have clearly arisen from interaction with popular views and moods. When he taught that Jerusalem would not be spared for the sake of a few saints – they would only save themselves (14.12–20) – he was no doubt countering those who could not believe that the city of David and of other friends of God could ever be destroyed. When he taught that each generation would itself be treated as responsible before God (ch. 18), he was arguing with those who said the present generation was hopelessly bound by the faults of former generations; he was insisting 'You can turn, you are free to repent, and God will accept you for yourselves.'

In this last example it is noticeable how Ezekiel gives a prophetic message, but uses the priestly style of argument from case-law: 'In the case where a man is righteous . . . In the case where such a man has a son who is a robber . . . But in the case where the son himself does not do as his father did . . . that man shall surely live . . . Cast away from you all the sins you have committed against me and get yourself a new heart and a new spirit! Why will you die, O house of Israel?'

Grace – the ground of hope

In spite of the legal style which often came into Ezekiel's arguments, he saw the hope of the revival of God's people and world as resting on God's initiative and good will. God would save his people for the sake of his holy 'name' – the outflow of his very nature. This 'name' was the revelation of the Lord, whereby he was known and called upon. When he hallows and sanctifies his name (asserts and reveals his divine nature and power), he comes with open might to rectify the situation of his people and world. The sin and suffering embodied in the Exile are a contradiction of the beauty and glory of the Creator's purpose, a violation of the holiness of his name. So now, not for the merit of Israel, but 'for the sake of my holy name, I am about to act, and I will show forth the holiness of my great name which you have profaned, and the nations will know that I am Yahweh' (36.22– 23).

The salvation springing from grace is further pictured as a sprinkling and washing and the creation of a new heart and spirit in the people, producing a new life of obedience, a united people dwelling in the promised land around God's Presence in the temple and under David or his heir (36.24–28; 37.15–28).

Re-thinking the Lord's Prayer

Our prayer 'Hallowed be thy name', in line with Ezekiel's prophecy, should mean not 'May people honour your name' but 'Create your good kingdom by the mighty unfolding of your nature and will – glorify your name! Effect your will!' We would be asking for God's action, springing from God's nature. In the New Testament wording, it is the use of passive verbs out of reverence which somewhat veils this meaning for us.

When all seems utterly lost, God's miracle!

The mixture of priestly detail and prophetic force is notable also in the most striking of all Ezekiel's visions, the reconstitution of the ancient skeletons (37.1–14). From verse 11 we can conclude that the people were assembled for solemn worship where lamentation dominated. Commemorating the Exile and the destruction of the holy city, the lamenting prayer rose incessantly to heaven: 'We are like dried-out bones, no hope left, cut off from the world of life.'

Ezekiel, part of that gathering, now fell into a trance and felt himself carried by the divine Spirit-wind to a valley piled high with bones of the long-dead. The power of God works through the prophet's voice, the mighty Spirit-wind brings the dead back to life. Ezekiel comes out of his trance with God's answer to the lamenting congregation: he will give them new life, and they will know and believe in his saving power.

The story of the vision gave much to ponder. The skeletons had

---

For your consideration

Though Ezekiel's vision of the bones was about the renewal of the Israelite community, it has always seemed laden with still deeper hope. In the following passage from my *Interpreted By Love* (pp.120–21), I related it to situations of despair in the modern world. Do you think my application stays true to the underlying meaning?

The emaciated prisoners had seen their guards suddenly flee, and now here were people who meant kindness to them, and who would nurse them back to life. But for how many was it too late? The grim work of exploring the camp revealed the evidence of mass extermination. These were bones that could only witness to irreversible atrocities.

Yes, the rescued are only the few, so far as we can understand. For most, it seems, help comes too late.

But it was the Spirit, the divine Breath, that bore Ezekiel to his valley of vision, where the piled-up evidence of death was contradicted. And the same Spirit gives strength to the rescuers of this world, those who mean kindness, and make springs of salvation in the great deserts of suffering. By this Spirit comes the mysterious knowledge that it is not too late – for God. None of his dear ones, in life or death, can fall beyond his redeeming reach.

long fallen apart, the bones so dry that no vestige of life remained. But for the Lord it was not too late. The vision of miraculous reconstruction, from bones to bodies to people, signified that he could and would restore the utterly broken community.

Rebuilding the city around its true centre

For depth of charismatic vision set in a mass of ecclesiastical detail we can hardly better chapters 40–48. In a trance, Ezekiel observes as though from a high mountain how the society of Israel is to be reconstructed. He sees the ideal plan laid out beneath him, and is instructed by a heavenly messenger as to all the measurements and dispositions. At the centre is a new temple, and much is said about its courts, gates, rooms, furnishings, offerings and ministries. In orderly fashion around this centre, the people, made whole again in the twelve tribes, have their allotted territories. The elaborate visionary scene is like a mandala centred on a symbol of God. Most significant, therefore, are three references to this Presence:

(1) Ezekiel sees the 'glory' of God (*kabod*), a manifestation like that of the Chariot vision, return to dwell in the temple (43.1–9);

(2) he sees a stream flowing from the temple, down the Kidron Valley, to reach and heal the sterile Dead Sea – a symbol of the ever-deepening grace that flows out from the Presence into the waste-land and turns death into life (47.1–12);

(3) the name of the new city is 'Yahweh Shammah', 'The Lord is there' (48.35).

Underlying the vision of the stream flowing from the new temple is memory of the situation of the old temple. Near the base of the hill bearing Solomon's temple, on the eastern side, the spring Gihon filled a pool, and also sent currents through passages under the city and along a course beside the city to some gardens. Moreover, in the wet winter, the Kidron valley below the east wall ran with water till its banks awoke to vivid green. For worshippers in the old days it had seemed a sign of life from the Creator's throne (Ps. 46.4–7).

All this lives again, and with marvellous transformation, in the vision of chapter 47. From the renewed Presence of God in the new temple, the entranced Ezekiel sees a stream of grace, a river of Paradise. We can appreciate the curious exactness of his depiction, reflecting his priestly training, if we can visit Jerusalem and look down on the Kidron Valley, especially after heavy rains. Down the course of the valley, as though waiting for the vision's fulfilment, monks were to settle. Where the ravine passes through grim desert a few miles from Bethlehem, early Christian hermits kept watch at Mar Saba. And where the gorge finally reaches the Dead Sea, Jewish monks of Qumran, around the time of Jesus, waited for that stream from the new Presence that would destroy death.

Ezekiel's spirituality – Spirit and regulation

In summary, we can say that Ezekiel's dedicated life helped his faith-community over a fearsome chasm in its history, and also had a great influence on future generations. He helped his people come to terms with their tragedy and prepare for reconstruction in hope of God's new creation.

But some of the concerns in his edited book and much of the detail seem strange to us. Here we have much to ponder about his combination of the Spirit with rules and regulations – his blend of the prophetic and the priestly. Throughout the history of religion the dilemma recurs. The visionary insights and impulses have to take effect in earthly circumstances, and large ideas have to be grounded in complex details. The prophet in Ezekiel saw visions which brought redeeming hope and kindled enthusiasm, while the priest in Ezekiel took responsibility for administering daily life in relation to the divine holiness.

In any case, the spiritual force of Ezekiel's visions is proved by the taking up of his New Jerusalem into the New Testament's Book of Revelation (Rev. 4; 5; 21; 22) and by the schools of mystics down the centuries who have meditated on his experience of the Chariot of God (the Merkaba).

A hermit's prayer answered in the Kidron Valley

It was said that Saint Sebas (=Mar Saba) was directed by an angel in 478CE to a desert site in the Kidron Valley for his cave and monastery. As the circle of hermits grew, there was difficulty in getting enough water. But while the good man prayed earnestly in a night of full moon, he heard a strange sound from the valley below. Leaning out from the precarious oratory, he saw a wild donkey digging with her hooves deep in the gravel of the valley-bed, then drinking long. He climbed down and found a source of water at the base of the cliff, which proved to be a never-failing supply. The monastery indeed has been able to survive to the present day. (See Chitty, *The Desert a City*, p.106.)

For discussion or writing

– Why is the call of Ezekiel recounted in such detail?

– How is holiness understood in the Book of Ezekiel?

– Compare Ezekiel's sense of ethical standards (ch. 18 etc) with that of Amos or Isaiah.

THE VOICE OF SECOND ISAIAH

Comfort, oh comfort my people, says your God,
speak to the sad heart of Jerusalem, cry to her
that her bondage is completed, her iniquity pardoned! (40.1–2).

You are my witnesses, says the Lord,
    my servants whom I have chosen
to know and believe in me
    and perceive that I AM HE (43.10–11).

Thus says the Lord to his anointed one, Cyrus,
    whom he has taken by the right hand,
to subdue nations before him
    and ungird the loins of kings . . .
I call you by name and give you titles
    though you have not known me (45.1–4).

When the heavens have vanished like smoke,
    and the earth has worn out like a garment,
        and its inhabitants have died like flies,
my salvation will remain for ever
    and my good purpose will not be frustrated (51.6).

He was abused and tormented
    but he did not open his mouth.
He was led like a lamb to the slaughter,
    and like a sheep silent before her shearers
        he did not open his mouth . . .
For the Lord had willed to crush him with suffering.
    Truly his soul made an offering for sin.
He shall see descendants, he shall live long,
    and in his hand the will of the Lord shall prosper (53.7,10).

How beautiful upon the mountains
    the feet of the bearer of tidings,
who cries, All is well!
    and carries good news and shouts, Victory!
and calls to Zion, Your God reigns! (52.7).

12

Second Isaiah – A New Song
for the Dawn

A cycle of song-prophecies

The prophet Isaiah was called in 742 BCE and served for over forty years. But the sixty-six chapters that stand under his name reveal backgrounds stretching over at least two and a half centuries. In this great assemblage, chapters 40–55 form a distinct block, a cycle of song-like prophecies, for the most part with a clear background in the late Babylonian Exile, 550–540 BCE.

There are signs, however, that they have not been placed in the book arbitrarily. Threads of continuity run through the book, so that it can be seen as basically the deposit of one long tradition of prophesying. It would be the work of the circle originated by Isaiah, a continuing fellowship with some function of lyrical prophecy in worship at the temple. The later generations of the fellowship, exiled to Babylonia, would still have been able to prophesy in their traditional style, telling of God's new work in history with language drawn from the old advent processions, ceremonies of atonement etc.

The eloquence of chapters 40–55 may justify us in thinking of one outstanding prophet-poet, the 'Second Isaiah' or 'Deutero-Isaiah' of our text-books, but we may do well to think of him as the leader of a prophetic circle, and so sometimes accompanied by other voices.

A *time for hope*

The historical setting of our cycle is the period just before the Persian conqueror Cyrus overwhelmed the Babylonian empire, and so about 550–540. He is actually mentioned twice in 44.24–45.7 and may be in mind in 41.25 and 46.8–13. His rise had already resulted in a great arc of empire from central Asia to Asia Minor, overshadowing the none-too-healthy empire of Babylon. As in earlier centuries, Hebrew prophets were sensitive to impending upheavals in the world order. On this occasion their message could be of good tidings for the exiles in Babylonia.

Redeemer

In Isa. 40–55 God is often called 'Redeemer'. The Hebrew word in question, *go'el*, was a legal term for a person closely related to you who would help you in need – he might release you from bondage due to debt, or even avenge your murder. Applied to God, the term speaks of his closeness in love and obligation, his readiness and power to free his people from the bonds of their troubles. Examples can be found in 41.14; 43.14; 44.6, 24; 48.17; 49.7. It is used with reference to the need of an individual in Ps. 19.14 and Job 19.25. The verb to 'redeem' is used in Ex. 6.6 and 15.13.

An *Old Testament gospel*

A gospel is a bringing of good news, the proclamation of peace, the announcing of salvation and the new reign of God (52.7). Such was the fundamental thrust of this cycle of prophecies, and all expressed in a vibrant singing style. It is declared that the sins that occasioned the Exile have now been amply atoned for, and the Lord will make procession with his people back to their land.

To a certain extent, the homeward procession is like a new Exodus: God again acts as 'redeemer' and the route is imagined through the desert. But this new journey is the procession of God and people to the holy centre of Zion/Jerusalem (established several centuries after the Exodus) and will have features of the advent processions of Jerusalem's pre-exilic festivals (as we shall see especially in ch. 52). There is a wonderfully spacious view here, inherited from the old festivals, which we must not overlook: the procession proclaims the shining forth of God's cosmic kingship, his ideal reign over all the world.

Occasions of the prophesying

Can we envisage more closely the occasions when the prophecies were uttered? There are three helpful indications. Firstly we have echoes of the sort of lamenting prayer we met in Ezek. 37. From Isa. 40.27 and 49.14, therefore, we can picture an assembly for commemorative worship, no doubt again at the water's edge. Complaining prayer would rise to God, and prophets might be moved to bring back an answer.

For your research

In order to sample the psalm-like quality of Second Isaiah, can you match each of these Isaiah passages with one of the Psalm passages?

| Isa. 40.31; | Isa. 42.10; | Isa. 52.7–8 |
| Ps. 96.1; | Ps. 96.10–13; | Ps. 103.5 |

Secondly, we can deduce from the themes of atonement and the processional entry of Yahweh as king, shepherd and saviour, that the occasion was the season of the autumnal new year. This had been the time of Jerusalem's chief holy days – New Year, Atonement and Tabernacles (/Booths/Ingathering). It was a time which even in the Exile could never be forgotten.

Thirdly, there are signs of dispute between prophets and people. It is clear that our prophets' gospel was not well received. Hopes had been dashed before, and through the long years faith had faded. So we picture our prophetic circle in a situation of dialogue with the people. With rising eloquence, against all objections, they reiterate their message of the enduring love of God and of his power as sole Creator, a power to dispose of the greatest nations and make all things new.

A glimpse of exilic worship

The lament of the worshippers:

Yahweh has forsaken me,
yes, the Lord has forgotten me.

God's reply through the prophet:

Would a woman forget her baby,
not feel for the son of her womb?
If ever they could forget,
still I should not forget you (Isa.49.14–15).

Yahweh's Servant: possibilities of interpretation

In addition to the main gospel of return and restoration and the arguments to counter disbelief, there is another great element in the message. It is the theme of the Lord's 'Servant', most distinctively expressed in 52.13–53.12, but appearing also (as many modern scholars have thought) in 42.1–9, 49.1–6, and 50.4–11. These passages are conveniently referred to as the four Servant Songs

A common interpretation is that this Servant is a figure or symbol for the nation. This view is based on the fact that in several other passages in Second Isaiah Yahweh calls Jacob/Israel (the ancestor who still lives in the nation) 'my Servant' (e.g. 41.8–9). Further support seems to come from the second Song, where the name 'Israel' is bestowed on Yahweh's Servant (49.3).

But on closer inspection these arguments are not strong. In contrast to the Servant of the Songs, Jacob-Israel (the ancestor in the nation) is not given a special mission, is sometimes severely blamed (e.g. 42.18–20; 48.4, 8) and may turn into a clear plural (48.1–2, 14–16; 42.18–25). When the name 'Israel' is bestowed on the Servant in 49.3, it cannot be to identify him as the nation, for he is immediately said to have a mission to the tribes of Israel (49.6). The name here seems rather to be a sign of his destiny and work, as with titles lavished on new rulers (e.g. Isa. 9.6). It would designate him as the true father of the nation, and also as a sign of God's triumph (Israel', in Hebrew *yisra-el,* meaning 'God reigns').

Another interpretation sees the Servant as identical with 'Second Isaiah', the prophet behind Isa. 40–55. At first sight this seems plausible in the second and third Songs, where the voice of the Servant is heard in the first person (49.1f.; 50.4f.). But the first and fourth Songs (42.1f.; 52.13f.) do not fit this line at all well. The forms and thought of all the Songs in fact bear little relation to materials about prophets. We never hear of a prophet being designated by God before others in such terms as 'Behold my Servant . . . I shall do such and such through him.' We never hear of prophets who are to be highly exalted as on a throne, sending forth rule to the nations of the world, releasing prisoners, receiving homage of kings, taking spoil as a conqueror. These considerations also tell against an interpretation of the Servant as a great prophet of the future, a second Moses.

The remaining possibility is the ancient and persisting interpretation that the Servant is a royal person, in some sense a ruler from David's line. Some think the prophecies were concerned with a historical figure, such as the cruelly exiled King Jehoiachin (cf. II Kings 25.27–29) or his grandson Zerubbabel (cf. Hag. 2.23). Others think of a more mysterious royal figure, a visionary hope that would fulfil the sure promises to David (Isa. 55.3).

This kind of 'messianic' interpretation has taken on a new force in the light of modern studies of the ancient royal ideal. It appears that in the festal ceremonies that regularly dramatized God's work as Creator, King and Saviour, there was also a presentation of the ideal mediating role of the Davidic king. The royal office was here set forth as the work of Yahweh's agent, bringing peace and justice to all the world. The ceremonies may even have shown an element of suffering in this ideal mission (perhaps reflected in Ps. 18, 22, 89, 101, 144), but this is less clear. The dramatic poetry from such pre-exilic ceremonies would have been known to the Second Isaiah circle, and so would have influenced the forms and themes of the Servant Songs.

This interpretation can claim to suit the context in Isa. 40–55 as a whole. The resultant picture is a natural unity: the gospel of the old festivals is now renewed and applied to the historical situation of the late Exile. God is to come as Creator-King to his royal city Zion, and will reign through his Davidic Servant, the agent of his salvation. It could be that the sufferings of the Exile have helped produce the extraordinary and creative emphasis on the Servant's ministry of suffering in chapter 53. But it is also possible that if more evidence of pre-exilic worship had been preserved, the great chapter might more obviously appear as a vision drawing on the insights of ancient liturgy.

All the interpretations that have now been outlined still have their advocates, as indeed do yet other views and variations. But the broad facts remain. Here, in a series of prophecies announcing the Lord's salvation for his people, his city and his world, emerges a figure through whose service salvation comes. This figure has royal features, but is not clearly identified.

The mysterious reticence seems to give him the freedom of times and spaces – an eternal validity, an appeal to every generation to discover for themselves, in their deepest beings, what is his meaning.

The study of 'forms' in Second Isaiah

In our chapter 'The Poetry and Patterns of Prophecy' (ch. 3 above), we noted that the prophets used 'forms', patterns and styles of public speech and chanted poetry that had evolved through many centuries, each pattern shaped by its appropriate purpose and setting. As we also noted, scholars have found that Isaiah 40–55 are chapters that lend themselves well to analysis into such 'forms'. Some seventy units have been picked out, many of which can be readily labelled as well-known traditional forms, while others can be reckoned as traditional forms although only one or two other examples have survived.

To explain the rich variety of forms in Second Isaiah, some think of an author able to draw from any situation (in general society, in education, in worship) and adapt freely for his purpose. But the range of forms does show special closeness to the psalmists and their poetry from worship. When we take into account the richness of the autumn festivals in royal Jerusalem (including processions, dialogue with God, coronations, and expressions of royal destiny), we begin to see that the forms in question could have developed there. They would then already have had a natural association with each other when our circle of prophets drew on them.

We can list these forms as follows:

(a) *Oracles of salvation* (e.g. 41.8-13, 14-16, 17-20). This form developed in the answers of God to laments in worship (cf. Ps. 12.5; 35.3; 60.6).

(b) *Hymns of praise* (e.g. 42.10-13; 44.23; 49.13; 52.7-10). This was the form for calls for praise in worship and often was responding to the sense of God's new presence in his power as Creator-King (cf. Ps. 96; 97; 98; 99). We may also note that fragments of hymnic form are very common in Second Isaiah, such as descriptions of God and his work (e.g. 42.5; 45.18; cf. Ps. 103.3-5; 104.2-4) and processional cries and depictions of processions (e.g. 40.3-5, 10-11; 52.8, 11-12; cf. Ps. 48.12-14; 68.4-6, 24-25; 98.10-13).

(c) *Legal speeches* (e.g. 41.1-5, 21-29). As in a court of law, Yahweh confronts rivals or pronounces sentence (cf. Ps. 50; 82; Isa. 1.2).

(d) *More general disputations* (e.g. 40.12-31; 45.9-13). Yahweh or his prophet takes issue with the people in arguing, reasoning style (cf. Ps. 50.7-23; Job 38-39). There is some resemblance here to the style of the sage with his scholars, but the form was also at home in the give-and-take of worship, as we see from Ps. 50 and Mal. 2.13-17; 3.6-18.

(e) *Prophecy striking at a foreign tyrant* (46.1-2; 47). This form uses irony and mocking address in foreseeing the enemy's downfall. Like the prophet's symbolic acts, the words are felt to be laden with Yahweh's power of doom (cf. Nahum 2–3; Jer. 50–51).

(f) *Oracles of royal calling* (42.1–4, 5–9; 49.8–12; 52.13–15). In this form God announces his choice of a ruler and bestows destiny and powers (cf. Ps. 2.7–9; 110; Isa. 9.6–7; I Sam. 9.17; 10.1).

(g) *Speeches of response by the designated leader* (49.1–7 50.4–9). The chosen one speaks of the task Yahweh has given him, testifies to his grace, and admonishes foes (cf. Ps. 2 and possibly also 4 and 62).

(h) *Choral exposition of the leader's mysterious destiny* (53.1–10). A group chants an explanation of his humiliation and exaltation (cf. Ps. 118.22–27 and the choral form in Ps. 20.7–9; 132.6–7; 144.12–15).

(i) *Ridicule of other gods and their images* (44.9–20; 45.5–7). The unique godhead of Yahweh is affirmed, and the relative impotence of other deities is scathingly described (cf. Ps. 115.3–8; Jer. 10.6–10; Hab. 2.18–20).

A question to consider

Is the biblical ridicule of images fair?

Sitting with the hearers of Second Isaiah

The foregoing pages have pointed to a way in which we could in imagination join those who heard the Isaiah prophets in the Exile. It will be well worth our while now to take this way. It is a way which leads us from mud brick houses down to the water-side, where groups are to maintain vigils and prayers for many days, stretching through the traditional holy season of New Year, Atonement, and Tabernacles. Forty years have not eased the pain of deprivation. Instead of the old festal rejoicing in the presence of

God, here is little but lamentation. Our way indeed is hidden from the Lord (40.27).

But one dimension of the old holy days can and does live again for us – the word and vision of the prophets. To our astonishment our complaint begins to be answered by an elderly prophet and his circle. There begins to stream from them an evocative poetry that would create a new era, a turn of destiny. The joy of the former festivals is kindled again as the prophets announce that sins have been purged, and Yahweh approaches along his holy route – 'Behold your God!' To the doubting, the prophets portray the incomparable power of the Lord who measured out all earth's waters in the hollow of his hand, and to whom the nations are but a drop from a bucket. We hear of his calling out every star by name, of his unsearchable wisdom, his unflagging strength, and his tender help to the weary who wait trustingly for him (ch.40).

But it is hard for us to escape the reality of the mighty city, empire and gods of Babylon. So the great prophet has us picture a judgment scene where rival divine claims are to be tried. The argument for Yahweh is that it is he who is giving the victory to the 'one from the east', to Cyrus the Persian. Images fastened with nails aptly represent the helpless gods, while the Lord declares, 'I Yahweh, the first and with the last, I AM HE (41.1–4).

And there is a word of encouragement for our father Jacob-Israel, who still lives in us, the national soul: 'You are my chosen Servant. Fear not! You lament that you are despised as a worm, but soon you will be like a threshing sledge, able to break down mountains of difficulties' (41.8–16).

As the days go by, it seems that further episodes of the old festivals live again through the prophetic vision, and prompt great hopes for the future. As Yahweh renews his kingly rule, the one who is to be a channel of that rule is prepared before him. This royal mediator is not identified, but it is for us a vital assurance to know that he is made ready before God and his mission and success established. It means much to us even to catch a glimpse of the Saviour-Servant, gifted with the Spirit, with quiet strength, with compassion and perseverance, to establish justice in all the earth, freeing the prisoners, shedding God's light (42.1–9).

The prophet renews tones of the old hymns, filled with a vision of God as mighty to save (42.10–17). But the old counterpoint of lament and re-assurance is also aptly revived. We speak as those who have long felt ourselves a people robbed and plundered, trapped in holes, while God would not hear or see. We are chided that we are the ones who would not hear or see, we, Israel, God's obtuse and disobedient servant and messenger. The dispute of God and people continues for some time, with the note of new forgiveness and promise sounding out again and again. We hear again that Cyrus will be God's instrument of change, and that Israel's life will be quickened: 'I will pour water on the thirsty ground and my Spirit upon your offspring.' We feel reassured to hear powerful words spoken for the doom of Babylon, but chastened again to be characterized as rebellious from birth, with a neck of iron and a forehead of brass (42.18–48.22).

There comes a day when the role of God's royal Servant is brought forward again, and it is revealed that his mission will be not only to regather the scattered tribes of Israel, but also to bring salvation to all nations. The revelation is conveyed in the dramatic manner of the old festival ceremonies. The prophet carries the Servant's voice, speaking to the whole world of his calling and mission. There is reflection on exhausting and fruitless labours of the past, as though the Davidic dynasty itself, its very soul, could speak through this representative. And the voice of the Lord is also carried, with strong promises and confirmation that his Servant will himself be 'a covenant for the people', embodying the bond with God, setting the captives free (49.1–13).

From now on we hear the note of promise ever stronger. The Lord declares his unfailing love for Zion, surpassing the strongest human bond. He will restore her children and give her supremacy as the seat of his reign. There has been no divorce from his bride Zion, and he is free to redeem the captives (49.14–50.3).

With the promises the theme of the way of suffering still re-appears. If we fear the Lord, so the prophet tells us, we must hear the voice of his Servant. This voice carried by the prophet speaks to us of a ministry of encouragement, sustaining the weary with the word of God, ever open to blows of scorn, confident in victory from the Lord (50.4-11).

On one exciting day, the prophet addresses us as 'pursuers of salvation, seekers of Yahweh' and gives promises of God's new reign that will make Zion his garden of paradise. Sharply the prophet evokes the action of God and summons Zion to arise from the dust (51.1-52.2)

And now unfolds a vision of procession – the Lord as king, leading his people into his holy city. He comes in as victor, preceded by runners who carry the good news. The ancient ceremonial lives again, and betokens the return from exile (52.7-12).

In this climax of the Lord's kingship, what of the role of the mediator, the Lord's Servant? The greatest word is now given on this, again in dramatic form. First it is the voice of the Lord: 'Behold, my Servant shall triumph . . .' High enthroned, anointed to a glory above mankind, God's priest-king to purify all nations – such will be the Servant on completion of his ordeal (52.13-15).

The prophets then tell of this ordeal. The Servant had first to appear without royal honour or beauty, scorned, shunned as a person with plague. He seemed to have earned divine punishment, yet, as the prophets reveal, he was bearing our sins, patiently suffering for others, himself without offence. Persecuted and put to death, he was buried as a sinner. But the oracles of exaltation ring out again. Because the Servant has made his life a sacrifice, and because of his 'knowledge', his closeness to God's heart, he will live and see with joy the fruit of his work – the restoration of multitudes to right relation with God. Such will be his victory and his triumph (53.1-12).

With awe, not fully comprehending, we hear the prophets' presentation of the mystery. Their story sounds like a timeless parable. Is it the destiny of the soul of the royal house, gathering in the sufferings of the young kings of the Exile? Is it a destiny still to be enacted? At least we know that here is further promise of the triumph of God's kingdom, and a special hope of forgiveness and restored relationship.

The colourful, dramatic prophecies continue, renewing the joy of former festivals. Zion's sorrow has been like that of a wife barren and forsaken. The prophet calls on her now to sing and to prepare for a large family – 'For your maker is your husband, the Holy One of Israel your redeemer.' 'The mountains may depart, but my love shall not depart from you' (ch. 54).

At the old festivals there were shared meals, food and drink blessed by God, vital power to make the souls of the worshippers truly live. Rising above our present deprivation, the visionary prophets are calling us to the feast of the Lord. They offer us a sustenance money cannot buy – the grace of the covenant, the bond with the Lord. It is the covenant in which 'David', the royal soul, the enduring mediator, leads the people into the promises of God. In his work as God's witness and guide for the nations, we too are called to have a part. And in all this feast created by the prophets' vision, the Lord once more is close, and we are invited to bring our prayers and correct our ways (55.1–9).

But the holy days, with their meetings by the water's edge, have now run their course. A final word from the great prophet assures us of the fulfilment of all that has been spoken. None of it, he says, will return to the Lord fruitless. The end will be universal joy. We shall be led forth with peace, the very mountains singing, and the trees clapping their hands (55.10–13).

A little while passes, and some of us are setting out on the long journey to Jerusalem. Many others of us prefer to hold on to the life we have in a foreign land. But we all have something to keep from that inspiration of the Isaiah prophets. For a while, as they chanted, the kingdom became real about us. We were touched by the splendour of our approaching Lord, by his forgiveness, by the triumph of right and faithfulness. In times of need the scenes will often live again for us – the highway of God through the wastelands, the divine shepherd gently carrying the lambs, the royal life offered in sacrifice, the feast of grace, the dancing trees and hills. Then we hope again and believe in the Lord and his Servant.

Poetry's depths and the Man of Sorrows

In the preceding section we have tried to feel the impact of Isaiah 40–55 as a whole. How difficult it is to comprehend its riches! Yet the cycle, by its very nature, ever prompts us to attempt it. More than any other stretch of prophecy, it captivates our hearts and attention. The chapters are loved for their bounding eloquence, their glowing hope, and their presentation of God as Creator and faithful Lord, but perhaps even more for their unique presentation of the atoning Saviour. Here is one who interposes himself to make multitudes right with God, one who 'bears our sins', wounded for our healing, dying that we may live, raised to enduring triumph because of his willing sacrifice.

Some point out inconsistencies. In 40.2 it is said that Jerusalem's iniquity has been atoned for, since she has received from the Lord's hand ample for all her sins. And the argument that it is only right that sinners should suffer for their own sins seems supported by Ezekiel (14.12–20; 18.20). But the thoughts and insights of the cycle should not be treated systematically, still less legalistically. We do not have here the balanced-up, worked-through theology that comes characteristically to European thinkers. What we have is poetry, penetrating visions of the eyes of the heart, each valid in its own context of experience. Such poetry sees through to depths unattainable by systematic thought. Insights are given here which are withheld from the mastering mind.

The great prophets, seeing deeply, declared that Jerusalem's tragedy had been brought on by her own sin (Isa. 50.1). The terrible destruction and the long, long years of exile could then well be seen as ample punishment, now to be succeeded by reconciliation and restoration (40.2). But at a still deeper level there was, and always in this world is, the need of one who brings divine grace to overcome the persistently alienating sin which defeats us on our own, one who 'bears' or 'takes away' the sin of the world, and makes us right, at peace with God. It is at this profound and universal level that the vision of the suffering Servant speaks.

Such poetry is prophecy because it glimpses eternal truth, truth which in its right time may more fully be manifested. The vision of the sacrificial Servant leaves little trace in the rest of Hebrew scriptures. There may be a link, as we shall see, in Isa. 61.1–3, in Zech. 9.9 and 13.7–9, and in Dan. 12.3. It is in the story of Jesus that it has seemed to come into its own, and so has taken an immense part in Christian faith and experience. In its Isaiah context, as we have seen, the figure is anonymous, and whether past, present or future can hardly be made out. It is almost as if this servanthood were an idea – but a divine idea, a revelation of Logos, creative Word from the heart of God; an idea that can clothe itself in many a person, in many a time, but which has one supreme embodiment that sends its light of sacrificial love to the beginning and end of the world, and recognizes all in whom the light shines as its own.

The theme in the passage is expressed clearly enough, even reiterated. Questions of meaning, however, arise in some details, and so I offer the following translation.

Some points in the translation

In 52.14 'him' is found in ancient translations, though our Hebrew has 'you'. 'I have anointed' (instead of the awkward 'marring' reflected in most of our versions) has support in the great Isaiah scroll from the Dead Sea caves (only a slight difference of spelling is involved) and matches the wording of Ps. 45.7. In 52.15 'asperge/purify' (rather than 'startle' or the like) has support in the usual sense of this verb and would indicate sacred authority. In 53.8 'rank' is a possible meaning which fits better than the usual 'generation'. 'His' rather than 'my (people)' is offered by the Dead Sea scroll. In 53.9 the usual meaning 'rich man' does not fit the preceding parallel line or the general context; a possible sense, in the light of Arabic, is 'corrupt/outcast'. In 53.11 'knowledge' could indicate intimacy with God, harmony with his will; an attractive alternative translation 'humiliation' has recently been severely questioned.

Opening oracle: assurance of the Servant's victory

52.13   See, my Servant shall be triumphant,
        he shall be very high, exalted, supreme.

14   Though many were appalled at him,
        yet I have anointed his face above men
        and his form above mankind.

15 So he shall purify many nations
　　while kings shut their mouths before him,
　for things never told they see
　　and things unheard of they contemplate.

Choral unfolding of the mystery

53.1 Who can believe our revelation,
　　to whom is the working of the Lord disclosed?

2 For he grew up like a shoot before him,
　　like a slip from arid ground.
　He had no beauty, no majesty
　　for us to look and admire him,
　　no features that we should desire him.

3 He was scorned and avoided by people,
　　a man of sorrows, familiar with injury.
　Like one from whom all hide their face
　　he was scorned and we disdained him.

4 But the ailments he bore were ours,
　　ours were the torments he carried.
　While we thought him plagued,
　　smitten by God and punished,

5 it was in truth for our sins he was pierced,
　　for our misdeeds crushed.
　On him fell the punishment for our well-being
　　and through his wounds came healing for us.

6 We had all strayed like a flock,
　　we had all gone our own way,
　but the Lord laid on him
　　the fault of all of us.

7 He was ill-treated and abused,
　　but he did not open his mouth.
　He was led like a lamb to the slaughter,
　　and like a sheep silent before her shearers
　　he did not open his mouth.

8   Of power and rule he was deprived,
      and who gave heed to his rank?
    He was cut off from the land of the living,
      for the sin of his people he was stricken.

9   And he was given his grave with the wrong-doers,
      and his burial-mound with the outcast
    though he had done no harm
    and there was no wrong in his mouth.

10   For the Lord had willed to crush him with suffering –
      truly his soul made an offering for sin.

Concluding oracle: the Servant will live, victorious

    He shall see his descendants, long shall he live,
      and by his work the will of the Lord shall prosper.

11   The outcome of his soul's pain he shall see
      and be satisfied.

    By his knowledge the Righteous One makes right,
      yes, he rights the multitudes,
    for their guilt he has borne.

12   Therefore I give him the multitudes as his share,
      and the masses he may take as his spoil,
    in reward for exposing his soul to death
      and being numbered with sinners,
    though truly he bore the sin of multitudes
    and for sinners he interposed himself.

Seeing into the heart of things

In his useful work *The Suffering Servant in Deutero-Isaiah* (pp.211–12), C.R.North cited these words of the respected theologian W.F. Lofthouse:

To my mind we can best find in the picture (of the Suffering Servant) the report of a moment of heightened consciousness, so tense and clear that we begin to see, as it were, into the heart of things. It is not a piece of history, biography, or autobiography . . . Five centuries before Calvary, the enigma of the cross was seen, and understood.

For discussion or writing

– How suitable are chs. 40 and 55 as introduction and conclusion of Isa. 40–55? How do they relate to each other?

– How important is the world (rather than just Israel) in the message of Isa. 40–55?

– Why do we hear so much of Zion in Isa. 40–55? What are the main features of the passages that address or refer to Zion?

THE VOICES OF HAGGAI, THIRD ISAIAH
AND MALACHI

You looked for a plentiful crop – see how meagre it is!
   Even as you gather it in I blow it away!
Why? asks the Lord of Hosts. Because my house lies in ruins
   while you run after your own houses.
Because of you the skies hold back their dew
   and the earth her yield (Hag. 1.9–10).

My house shall be called the house of prayer for all peoples.
The Lord who gathers Israel's outcasts says,
   I will gather others to them beside their own gathered ones
                                        (Isa. 56.7–8).

Is not this the fast I choose –
   to loosen cruel bands and unfasten the thongs of the yoke,
   to let the oppressed go free and break off every yoke,
   to share your bread among the starving,
   and bring the homeless into your home? (Isa. 58.6–7).

See, I am creating new heavens and a new earth!
Old sufferings shall not be remembered . . . or rise up in the heart.
   Be glad, rejoice for evermore in what I now create!
                                        (Isa. 65.17–18).

To (the ancestor of the priests) I entrusted Life and Peace.
   I gave him reverence and he revered me
      and held my name in awe.
Teaching of truth was in his mouth . . .
   and he brought back many from wrong-doing.
For the lips of a priest should guard knowledge (of God) . . .
   for he is the messenger of the Lord of Hosts (Mal. 2.5–7).

Have we not all one father,
   has not one God created us?
So why are we faithless to each other,
   breaking the covenant handed down to us? (Mal. 2.10).

On you who fear my name
   shall rise a sun of righteousness
   with healing in her wings (Mal. 4.2).

13

Haggai, Third Isaiah, Malachi – Courage to Rebuild

A new regime – permission to rebuild

In 539 Cyrus the Persian swallowed up the Babylonian empire. The Holy Land was now to remain within the vast Persian empire till the arrival of Alexander the Great in 333. Almost immediately, in 538, Cyrus seems to have allowed the Jewish exiles freedom to return home, and he also decreed the rebuilding of the temple.

The returning was not such a glorious matter. After fifty years

---

Cyrus the restorer of nations and temples

In Ezra 1.2–4 is preserved in Hebrew the gist of a royal *proclamation* that will have been made by criers and by written notices where the exiles lived. Ezra 6.3–5, on the other hand, preserves a *memorandum* in the administrative language, Aramaic, the official record of Cyrus's oral decision.

The reliability of these materials is supported by the discovery of an inscription on a clay barrel where Cyrus, for the benefit of the Babylonians, relates how their god Marduk, 'king of the gods', chose him as a righteous ruler for the world. Hence he has entered Babylon without a battle, restored deported peoples to their homelands and rebuilt their temples.

(The inscription is given in Pritchard (ed), *Ancient Near Eastern Texts*, pp.315–16.)

or more of exile, some Jews had better prospects in Babylonia than in returning to try to find a niche in the society that had continued in the Holy Land. Those who did return had many problems in re-establishing themselves. But at least the Persians were relatively benign. They ruled through native governors of districts, and in Jerusalem we hear of a governor Zerubbabel ('Begotten-in-Babylon'), grandson of King Jehoiachin, and beside him a 'high priest' Joshua.

A snapshot of history

The little book of Haggai gives us a glimpse of the situation in Jerusalem after the end of the Exile. Seventeen years have passed since Cyrus authorized the rebuilding of the temple, and now, in 521, it is clear that little progress has been made. Conditions are difficult, not least because of poor harvests.

A recent crisis for the unity of the Persian empire may have stimulated the prophets. Haggai relays God's word as critical of those who give much care to their own dwellings, while neglecting the building of the house of the Lord. He links the bad harvests with this failure to see to the conduct of worship.

Supported by the prophet Zechariah, Haggai was successful in arousing action, and in 515 the new temple came into service. The elderly wept to see how poorly it compared with the first temple.

What would Haggai say today?

Here is a suggestion:

> Do what you can for the glory of God, however inadequate your work. If his Spirit is with you (cf. Hag. 1.13; 2.4–5) it will be enough. God will know the right time to take up your work, perfect it, and make it bear fruit.

Can you make a different suggestion, in about 50 words?

But Haggai continued to encourage. Though God's blessings might still be held back by the people's sinfulness, which could still impair their worship, the new temple was a turning point for hope (2.10–19).

So Haggai foretold a time of splendour through a great action of God. Zerubbabel would be exalted as a great royal figure ('my Servant') to mediate God's authority, as though he were the signet-ring on God's finger. This specific form of hope for David's line was not in fact fulfilled.

Third Isaiah – end of a great tradition

We have already found some of the greatest works of prophecy collected under the name of Isaiah. The cycle of prophecies conveniently referred to as 'Second Isaiah' (Isa. 40–55) reflected the situation in Babylonia about 550–540. Close to this cycle in date, and often in style, is the last section of the book (Isa. 56–66), conveniently referred to as 'Third Isaiah'.

For the most part, these concluding chapters reflect conditions in Jerusalem in the early decades of Persian rule. Chapters 60–62 remind us of Second Isaiah's style, and so support the idea that a particular prophetic fellowship, descended from Isaiah's circle, endured the Exile and then was able to return to Jerusalem. Some of the materials may indeed have been handed down from early in the Exile (63.18; 64.11).

The materials of this collection are quite varied. Around the glowing promises of chapters 60–62 are placed sharp criticisms of leading classes, lamenting prayers to God, striking teachings, and visions of divine judgment.

Criticism of the post-exilic community

The tensions and problems of this period of difficult restoration are well reflected in several sharp attacks by Third Isaiah prophets. They condemn those with special responsibility for society's welfare as driven by greed; no longer sensitive to the plight of the needy, these leaders are like over-fed, slumbering watchdogs (56.10–12). The wealthy treat the poor callously (58.6–7; 59.1–8; 61.1).

There is also condemnation of recourse to strange cults (57.3–13); these would be rife in a time of deep foreign penetration and much religious confusion. Neglect of the Sabbath (56.2; 58.13–14) is also a sign of a community weak in religious unity and purpose.

Shafts of light

Some of the teaching in Third Isaiah is indeed surprisingly radical. While there is deep concern that the Sabbath be respected (56.2; 58.13–14), there is also a perception that a show of fasting may not be a priority in the Lord's eyes (58.1–14); and sacrifices at the temple without obedience are only a provocation (66.3–4). And though other prophets (especially Haggai) had reason to urge the completion of the new temple, here we have rather a reminder of the Lord's freedom and transcendence, his greatness beyond all earthly structures (57.15; 63.15; 66.1–2). And while some inherited laws prohibited foreigners and eunuchs from the holy spaces of the temple, these inspired prophets bring an overruling word of the Lord welcoming these outcasts (56.3–8; 66.18–21; contrast Num. 18.1–7; Ezek. 44.4–9, 15).

Far-reaching prophecy

In her book *Isaiah 56–66,* (pp.108–9), Grace Emmerson stresses deeply significant elements in Third Isaiah's thought:

These chapters affirm that the heart of true religion consists in putting into practice in daily living Yahweh's own commitment to social justice. It is no longer to be the privilege of birth and physical descent that ensures a place within the covenantal community, but personal commitment in obedience to God . . . The needs of individuals – eunuchs returned from royal service in exile, foreigners, the poor and oppressed – all these are taken into account.

Through all present difficulties, the bright hopes of Second Isaiah are rekindled (chs. 60–2). There is even a notable echo of the Servant Songs in 61.1–3, envisaging a royal mission, filled with the power of the Spirit of the Lord, to proclaim salvation to the lowly, bind up the broken-hearted, and break the shackles of the captives. Here we see again how the prophets of the Isaiah circle were apt to take up images and moments from the old festivals and declare their imminent realization in history. Their message reflects new year celebrations at the temple. After days of mournful penitence, the ashes and rags are to be put away. In bright garments, the pilgrims welcome their God, who comes to abase the arrogant and exalt the lowly.

Rather as in the second and third Servant Songs (Isa. 49 and 50) there is here a dramatic aspect, in that the prophet represents the voice of the royal saviour who will act for God. Like the ancient kings, this saviour receives the Spirit at his anointing and commissioning, and is especially responsible for the poor and oppressed. Like the kings, he has to witness for the Lord (cf. 55.4) and announce God's victory (cf. Ps. 40.9–10).

We can well imagine, then, that at some new year festival, when times were hard and spirits crushed, the prophet, in the manner of Second Isaiah, kindles the hope of salvation. There will be One to fulfil the office of the royal Servant of the Lord, One empowered to heal the broken hearts and throw open the prisons, announcing the new year of favour, the time of beauty and

---

For your research

Can you find chapter and verse for these phrases from an old translation of Third Isaiah?
– 'a house of prayer for all peoples'
– 'a garland for ashes'
– 'earth is my footstool'
– 'call the Sabbath a delight'
– 'nations shall come to thy light'

---

strength in communion with God. In expressing the very voice of the royal figure of his vision, the prophet brings the kingdom of God to the threshold of experience.

Malachi – late messages

The last book in the prophetic collection is that of Malachi. The contents have a background of Jerusalem around 480 BCE. While Judah has troubles on the southern borders with its neighbours the Edomites, there are troubles enough internally. Malachi denounces irreverent service of priests in the sanctuary, and then condemns sorcery, slowness to pay day-labourers, callous divorcing of wives, and oppression of widows, orphans and resident foreigners.

There is a remarkable glimpse of universal religion, implying criticism of Jerusalem's elitist but degenerate priesthood:

> From the rising of the sun to its setting
> my name is great among the nations
> and in every sanctuary incense is offered to my name,
>   says Yahweh of Hosts,
> but you (priests in Jerusalem) profane it (1.11–12).

Here the worship of the Creator, the 'God of heaven' exalted by the Persians throughout their vast empire, is set in contrast with that in Jerusalem. God would sooner have the former, says Malachi trenchantly, so lacking are the Jewish priests in awe, humility and integrity. It is not so much a theory of religions, as an expression of blazing indignation.

The Hebrew word *mal'ak* means 'one who undertakes an errand', hence 'angel' or 'messenger'. 'Malachi' means 'my messenger/angel'. We may wonder if the name was given to the prophet because of his message in 3.1–5, something of the angels mentioned there being seen in him. It may of course simply be that this collection of prophecies was at first anonymous, with a heading like that of the closely preceding Zech. 12.1, then subsequently supplied with a name from the word in 3.1, 'My messenger'. Whatever the explanation, there is now a fitting link between the man and his message. He who works for a vision already embodies it.

We have noticed in other prophetic books evidence of dialogue between God and people during a sacred assembly (for example in Second Isaiah). The Book of Malachi is notable in being built from six pieces of such dialogue. The basic pattern of this interchange begins with the prophet expressing a word of God, and continues with the people's response (an opposing query), then God's rejoinder, and then a concluding statement of God's position. A short example can be found in 1.2–5, while in 1.6–2.9 the pattern is extended as the priests query God a second time.

Although the interchange sounds somewhat truculent in these brief records, we may detect here a traditional procedure for eliciting the divine will. When the prophet, at a solemn assembly, has announced a word of God, the congregation's representatives – elders or priests – make a cautious or questioning response, as though testing the validity of the prophet's word. The prominence of this form here points to Malachi's character as a prophet serving in temple gatherings, but finding the people hard to convince.

Beyond present injustice

As in most of the prophetic books, so also in Malachi, consideration of present ills passes into expectation of God's great coming to bring justice. There are several imaginative features in this prophecy. In 3.1–5 two heavenly messengers seem to be involved. The first ('my messenger') is to clear the way before God; he is a kind of herald. The second ('the messenger of the covenant in whom you delight') is the guardian of the justice required by God's covenant, one who is able to secure restitution for those crushed by oppression.

Such angels are manifestations of the concern of the infinite divine power with the problems of one place and time. But their deeper significance is that in and with them the Lord is present and active. We have the sense that the imagination of heaven's rule in this period is influenced by experience of the immense and impressive Persian administration. From the palace in Susa, emissaries speeded to all parts of the empire, that stretched from the

Mediterranean to remotest Asia. Through these envoys the power and will of the great king of kings was realized in every place. And when the king himself came to set wrongs right, his intervention would be prepared and facilitated by specialist ministers.

Another feature of Persian government was its devotion to written records. The Book of Esther catches this trait in its story of the Persian king who, unable to sleep, browsed through the great royal diary in which the affairs of state were faithfully recorded, and so he was able to correct an injustice (Esth. 6). For Malachi it is a book of heavenly records that will ensure justice for God's people. The prophet is facing the bitter complaint that it is the evil-doer that Yahweh really approves (Mal. 2.17); it is useless to serve God, they say. for he prefers to bless the arrogant (3.13–15). Malachi's answer is that the righteousness of God will be fully clear in the great day of his coming, and in the meantime those who have feared the Lord – those who in practice heed his reality – are enrolled in a book of remembrance in heaven. Their faith will not be forgotten. They will be his special treasure on the day of his great action (3.16–18).

Concluding images: furnace and rising sun

Two notable images emphasize the distinction that will be apparent on that day (Mal. 4.1–3). The wicked will find the Lord's coming to be like the feeding of stubble to an oven. But for those who fear his name, acting according to his reality, it will be like the rising of the sun of justice and healing. The winged sun-disk (the rays having come to be represented as wings) was already an ancient and widespread symbol when it was used by the Persians to express healthful divine order channelled through their rule. It was certainly known to the Jews, for we find it on their jar-handles before the Exile, and on a fourth-century coin. Malachi uses this image evocatively to indicate the breaking forth of God's light of salvation to right wrongs and heal the suffering.

Two little passages then end the Book of Malachi and so also the whole prophetic collection. Indeed we have the impression that the book and the greater collection have already taken shape, and that the keepers of the tradition want here to add some final words.

First, then, we have an admonition to remember the law of God's servant Moses, given at Horeb (4.4). In fact this thought, in this form, is not typical of the prophetic books, but was becoming the focal point of Jewish religion around 400 BCE. So here we gain a glimpse of how the varied riches of Hebrew scripture are being drawn together, with the revelation to Moses being accorded the key position.

Last comes a reference to the other ancient prophet of towering prestige – Elijah (4.5–6), also associated with Mount Horeb (I Kings 19.8). It may be that discussion had continued as to the identity of the 'messenger' in 3.1 and that an answer was given in this passage: Elijah, said never to have died but to have been caught up into heaven (II Kings 2.11), would return to, prepare the people for the Lord's own coming. With the current state of society, with disruption reaching into the core of family relation-ships, there was danger that the earth would be doomed with a divine curse. But Elijah would return to reconcile parents and children to each other in time for the day of reckoning.

Thus the Book of Malachi, The Book of the Twelve ('minor') Prophets, and the whole collection of the Prophets all end with these brief references to the two themes that were to characterize Jewish religion through to New Testament times: The revelation to Moses (with its prescriptions for daily living that give shape and identity to the religious community) and the awe-filled expectation of the Lord's great coming with judgment and salvation.

For discussion or writing

– From Haggai, Third Isaiah and Malachi, what are the chief impressions we get of life in post-exilic Jerusalem?

– Discuss the symbolism of 'light', referring especially to Isa. 60.1–3 and Mal. 4.2.

– What thoughts arise from the fact, as noted above, that with its word *mal'ak* Hebrew does not make a distinction between a heavenly and a human 'angel/messenger'?

THE VOICES OF OBADIAH, JOEL AND ZECHARIAH

The arrogance of your heart has deceived you,
  you who dwell in the clefts of the mountains
    in your home in the heights,
thinking in your heart,
  Who can bring me down to earth?
Though you were high as the eagle,
  though you made your nest among the stars,
even from there I would bring you down,
  says the Lord (Obad. 3–4).

On all kinds of people I will pour out my Spirit,
  and your sons and daughters will prophesy,
your old men dream dreams,
  your young men see visions (Joel 2.28).

Multitudes, multitudes in the valley of decision!
  For the Day of the Lord is near in the valley of decision
                                          (Joel 3.14).

Not by force and not by power,
  but by my Spirit, says the Lord of Hosts (Zech. 4.6).

Old men and women shall again sit in Jerusalem's streets,
  leaning on their sticks for very age.
And the streets of the city will be full of boys and girls
  playing in her streets (Zech. 8.4–5).

Dance for joy, dear Zion,
  sing out, Jerusalem my daughter!
See, your king comes to you,
  proved righteous and clothed with salvation,
humble and riding on a donkey,
  on a colt, a donkey's foal . . .
He will decree peace to the nations,
  and his rule will stretch from sea to sea,
    and from the sacred river to the ends of the earth
                                          (Zech. 9.9–10).

14

Obadiah, Joel, Zechariah, Jonah – Varieties of Service

Obadiah – beyond the bitterness of treachery

Between the Dead Sea and the Gulf of Aqaba the Edomites lived in a rugged terrain, their cities hidden among cliffs, almost inacessible. Sometimes they had been ruled by the House of David, sometimes they achieved independence. When the Babylonians finally crushed the Jerusalem kingdom in 587, the Edomites were glad to assist the invaders and turn the tragedy of their brother people to their advantage.

The prophecy of Obadiah, probably soon afterwards, condemns this behaviour. Feeling themselves secure in their mountains, he says, they are guilty of arrogance (vv.3–4). Moreover, they have betrayed a covenant-partner, a brother, and must now expect themselves to be betrayed (5–14). The Lord will stir up nations to attack them in their turn (1).

Bitterness between adjacent peoples, such as was seen in our own day in the former Jugoslavia, is recognizable here. But then a deeper perspective opens (15–21). Obadiah declares that the Day of the Lord against all nations is near, and the Lord's own reign will be established. Although the thought is still nationalistic (17–21), at least it is connected to the greater prophetic vision of a salvation from Zion which is a divine reign of righteousness and peace.

That Obadiah belonged to a company of prophets is indicated by the opening words 'We have heard a revelation from the Lord' (v.1); in shared inspiration the circle has become aware of a stirring among the nations caused by an angelic 'messenger' sent out from the Lord's council. We may also note that a passage very similar to Obad. 1–9 has been preserved in Jer. 49.7–22; this suggests how prophets drew from and contributed to the tradition of the wider prophetic fellowship.

Joel – *when the moon turns to blood*

One may estimate Joel's date as shortly before or shortly after the Exile. A particular crisis again stirs up the sense of the nearness of the Lord. In this case the initial danger is a plague of locusts. The prophet first calls on leaders and people to recognize the urgency of the situation as the locusts strip the land of its crops and fruits. He calls for rites of penitence and prayer:

> Proclaim a fast, call a solemn assembly,
> gather the elders and inhabitants of the land
> to the house of Yahweh your God,
> and cry out to Yahweh! (1.14).

Soon Joel himself is leading the intercessions:

> The stores are desolate . . . the corn has failed.
> How the beasts groan, for they have no pasture!
> To you I cry, Yahweh, for fire has devoured
> the pastures of the wilderness . . . (1.15–20).

Then, speaking for God, Joel has more warnings to give. Let the ram's horn trumpets warn of attack, the approach of the Day of the Lord who comes with his terrible army (2.1–11)! The fearsome prospect should induce repentance:

> Yet even now return to me with all your heart . . .
> return to Yahweh your God
> for he is gracious and compassionate . . .
> Who knows if he may now relent again
> and leave behind him blessing? (2.12–14).

So the call for rites of penitence is renewed, and we have a vivid picture of how such worship used to proceed (2.15–17). The whole people, from the elderly to the infants, assemble in the temple courts with much weeping and wailing, while a priestly choir chants laments to move the Lord to pity.

It is then recorded that, when all this penitent worship was offered, the prophet heard a favourable answer from the Lord. The penitence was accepted and prophecies of plenty followed: 'Fear not, O soil . . . fear not, wild beasts . . . and you, children of Zion, rejoice . . .' (2.18–27).

The favourable message is then developed, with an accumulation of predictions (2.28–3.21). Terrible indeed will be the world judgment, the Day of the Lord, with wonderful and fearsome portents. 'On all flesh' – male and female, young and old, high and low – will fall the inspiring Spirit of God. By this gift of the Spirit, all will be able to see through the ordinary circumstances of life to the greater realities of God (2.28–29).

The Day of the Lord will bring requital on strong nations which abused God's people in their weakness. The Lord will dwell in Zion with a redeemed people (3.20–21), and a fountain of life will flow from the house of the Lord (3.18). Then all who call on the name of the Lord will be saved (2.31).

Thus we see that the Book of Joel is rich in material where ultimate issues shine through temporary crises. It has been striking also to see how concretely the book illustrates the close relation of prophetic ministry and great assemblies for worship.

The ministry of Zechariah

From a list of priestly families (Neh. 12.4, 16), it seems that Zechariah was among the priests who returned to Jerusalem soon after the Persians took control of the Babylonian empire. We glimpse here in his family circle the attitude of courage and hope which was to be the hall-mark of his ministry.

A clear indication of the date and concerns of Zechariah's ministry is given in the first part of the book, chs. 1–8. He began to prophesy in 520, two months after Haggai had uttered his first call for the rebuilding of the temple (he is coupled with Haggai in

Ezra 5.1 and 6.14, Neh. 12.16, and there called 'son of Iddo'; so his description in Zech. 1.1 as 'son of Berekiah, son of Iddo' may be a confusion from Isa. 8.2). He too was concerned with encouraging the community of Jerusalem and Judah in the difficult days of restoration after the Exile, and he looked for the rebuilding of the temple (6.15; 8.9) and the full salvation of Zion in a new kingdom of the Lord. Along with his promising words, he uttered calls for repentance and pure living.

There is a sudden flash of light on the historical situation when he gives an account of a remarkable symbolic action that he felt bidden to perform (6.9–14). In its original form this account seems to have described how Zechariah had to prepare a crown for the governor Zerubbabel, descendant of David, in promise of his future elevation to the throne, honoured as the builder of the new temple, the glorious branch from the ancient dynastic tree, with a representative of the priestly house beside him in peaceful accord. But events turned out differently. Zerubbabel soon disappears from the records, and the high priest moves into the top position as ruler under the Persians. It seems that our account was then revised, with the high priest's name rather awkwardly replacing Zerubbabel's in 6.11.

In 518 Zechariah was prompted to deliver weighty prophecies in response to an enquiry brought by delegates from the people of Bethel to the priests and prophets in Jerusalem (chs. 7–8). The question was whether the annual fasts commemorating the fall and destruction of Jerusalem in 587 should still be observed. Such services of lamentation were intended to move God to pity and restorative action, and now the Exile was over and work on the new temple begun in earnest, it might seem harmful to re-create those times of divine displeasure. Zechariah represented God as saying in reply, 'When you did all that, was it for me?' The Lord would be more impressed by justice, faithfulness, compassion, heartfelt and practical love for the needy and vulnerable (7.8). It was the renewal of an old message, a great message, which had not been heeded in the past. This was why the pleasant land had been made desolate; this was what now needed attention (7.11–14).

For your consideration

We sometimes wonder whether to modify or discontinue our own national ceremonies of commemoration. Would Zechariah's message ('Was it for me that you fasted these seventy years') still be relevant?

All the same, Zechariah was able to say that the Lord was full of zeal to restore Zion, the soul-centre of his people and the world (ch. 8.) The commemorative fasts would become seasons of joy. But the summons still stands: 'Love *emet* and *shalom*', cleave to faithful, wholesome ways for the common good (8.18–19). Among such a faithful people, the presence of the Lord would be so wonderfully known that other peoples would come to share in the worship and the blessings. And Zechariah pictures a Jew with ten Gentiles clinging to his robe and begging to be led to the presence of the Lord (8.20).

We thus have the impression of a prophet involved with the religious institutions in Jerusalem, but who was not one to give a pat answer when a cultic ruling was requested. Vexingly, he focussed on motives, on the deep and uncomfortable requirements of God. Encouraging, promising, he yet called relentlessly for the purification of motives and conduct in accordance with God's will for mercy, truth and peace.

Visions in the night

A unique feature of the records of Zechariah is the series of eight nocturnal visions (1.7–6.8). The prophet tells of strange things he sees in the night – red horses, weird flying objects, olive and myrtle trees, a golden lamp-stand, the seven eyes of God, and many other mysteries; and with the help of an angel-interpreter he finds in the visions messages for his people. There is some resemblance to the visions of the priest-prophet Ezekiel and some anticipation of the apocalyptic books (such as Daniel, treated in our next chapter).

In the first vision (1.7–17) the red, white and sorrel horses are the angelic patrols of God, which report that the nations are quiet and at ease. This may reflect the fact that the new Persian king, Darius I, had just defeated his rival and established his succession. In the preceding time of instability Hebrew prophets will have read signs of divine action that would lead to glorious restoration for Jerusalem and David's line. Now hopes are dashed, and the lament goes up, 'How long, O Lord?' The answer is re-affirmation of the Lord's goodwill and purpose for his people. The temple *will* be rebuilt, and Jerusalem too.

The second vision (1.18–21) is of iron horns, denoting the military might of empires that had savaged Judah. Suddenly blacksmiths appear – angels sent by God to demolish the horns with hammer and fire.

In the third vision (2.1–5) a figure is seen going out to measure Jerusalem, the start of reconstruction, but angels run after him to say that no walls should be built. The people and their animals will be far too numerous to contain, and protection will be provided by God – his glory within, and a rampart of fire without.

In the gates of heaven, so the fourth vision showed (3.1–10), the Lord in the form of his angel presides over a trial. Joshua the high priest represents the people of Judah. He wears the dirty garb of the penitent, as the lamenting worshippers have done ever since the destruction of Jerusalem. The angelic prosecutor, the 'Satan' (meaning 'Adversary'), stands beside him to remind God of the people's guilt. But the penitential time is completed, and the Lord dismisses the accuser and commands that Joshua be clothed in the purity of priestly splendour. Then a stone is seen before Joshua; it has seven eyes and is to be inscribed by God as his own. This signifies the restoration of the temple and the ever-vigilant presence of God. There is promise too of the coming 'Branch', the great descendant of David. The priests will be blessed as God's intermediaries, but only if they walk in his ways.

Co-operation of the Davidic heir and the high priest is pictured also in the fifth vision (4.1–14). A gold lamp-stand appears, supporting seven saucer-lamps – the eyes of God's rule. A bowl on top of the stand feeds oil to the lamps, and on each side stands an olive tree, apparently to supply oil. Oil signifies the anointing whereby God empowers his royal and priestly servants, and the trees in fact stand for the two 'sons of oil', the coming king with his high priest. Within this mysterious prospect is enclosed a more definite word for the present governor Zerubbabel, grandson of King Jehoiachin. Not indeed by human power, but by God's Spirit he will be able to rebuild the temple. The mountain of difficulties – perhaps indeed the mountain of debris left by the old tragedy – will be cleared away and the crowning stone of the temple will be recovered to crown the new work.

And now appear strange Flying Objects, that will, however, be identified. Thus in the sixth vision (5.1–4) there comes flapping through the sky a giant scroll. In it are written curses against those who pollute the land, whether by thieving or by abusing the name of the Lord (oath-breakers and hypocrites). Its power will radiate into the houses of such deceivers, rotting timber and stone alike. And in the seventh vision (5.5–11) is seen a woman, thrust in a barrel and firmly fastened down with a lid of lead. She represents the wickedness that ruins the land (especially the fertility cults). Two witch-like figures take up the barrel and its occupant, and with the wind filling their deep sleeves, convey it through the sky to Babylon. Here is prepared a temple and podium suitable for this idol-goddess. These two visions of the Flying Objects thus predict the purifying of the Holy Land, when it will be made ready for the return of the divine Presence.

Finally in the eighth vision (6.1–8, 15), Zechariah sees again the great portals of heaven, which appear as two mountains of bronze. Four chariots dash out, drawn by horses respectively red, black, white, and dappled. Like the four winds, these storm over the whole earth, and through the north-bound chariot especially the Spirit-wind of God stirs up the dispersed Jews to return and help rebuild the temple. Typically for Zechariah, the series of visions concludes, 'And all this will come to pass if you sincerely obey the voice of the Lord your God' (6.15).

Altogether, Zechariah is a remarkable and distinctive prophet. He is a visionary close to the priesthood, somewhat like Ezekiel. Rather more fully than Haggai, he discloses to us the moods and hopes in Jerusalem early in the period of the Persian empire. The end of the Exile did not then seem such a complete turn to salvation. It had not even yet become clear that the period of punishment and penitence was over. The land seemed still defiled. The prophet saw much wrong done in society. But he also saw wonderful symbols of the saving and restoring work of God. He heard from heaven the voice of promise, bringing light and encouragement to those facing immediate and heavy tasks. But he never let the promises run too far ahead of the call for a pure and true way of life.

For your consideration

Which of Zechariah's night-visions do you find most interesting and imformative? Could you make it the core of a presentation for children?

Zechariah 9–14 and the king on a donkey

In these chapters the person of Zechariah and the people who surrounded him have disappeared from view. Although it may be possible to trace some continuity with Zechariah's favourite themes, the material has a rather different form and feeling. It is in fact difficult to locate historically, and may result from the use and development of ancient oracles by circles in the fifth and fourth centuries. Puzzling as it often is, it would be a pity to pass it by without noting examples of its imaginative power.

First we may take the prophecy of a coming saviour-king (9.9–10): 'Rejoice greatly, O damsel Zion . . . See, your king comes to you.' This king is humble and rides on a donkey. The war-horses, chariots and weapons are put away, and he declares peace to all nations and rules with the salvation of God from one end of the world to the other. Fine donkeys, covered with rich rugs, were an ancient mark of royalty, but the animal also came to signal peace, in contrast with the battle-trained cavalry and chariot horses. The prophecy may draw on a scene from the dramatic autumnal new-year ceremonies of ancient royal Jerusalem, interpreting it with urgent prophetic promise for the post-exilic, kingless city. The New Testament tells of symbolic enactment of the prophecy by Jesus, signifying that the time of the Messiah and his kingdom of peace has drawn nigh (Mark 11.1–10).

The stricken shepherd and the wounded prophet

We may note also some mysterious and evocative sayings in Zech. 11 and 13. First, the prophet acts out an allegory of how the Lord set out to care as a good shepherd for his flock Israel, but was provoked to abandon them (11.7–14). The allegory shows the Lord's care derided, as he is paid off with a derisory sum, thirty pieces of silver (11.12–13). The punishment of the people is symbolized as the prophet now takes the part of a bad shepherd who will not seek the straying sheep (11.15–17).

The doom of prophecy itself is envisaged in another evocative passage (13.2–6). The prophets have succumbed to an 'unclean spirit'. They will be so out of favour that they will try to conceal their identity. Their own parents will pierce them through. They will hide their prophetic mantles and claim that their wounds (from self-laceration in Canaanite-style prophetic dance, cf. I Kings 18.28) were received at a riotous party with friends.

Most evocative of all is the oracle in which the Lord calls to the sword to smite his shepherd. The Lord's royal Servant, his king, must die before the covenant of God and people can be restored (13.7–9). When the shepherd is slain, the sheep are scattered. Suffering engulfs the people, till a true remnant is refined from the furnace and pure communion with God is achieved.

Holy bells and saucepans

The book of Zechariah ends with more examples of prophecy in close touch with the temple and its rites, ministers and values.

Celebration of the Lord's kingship, the heart of the autumn festival, provides the image for the new world which is sensed as near at hand. The Lord will then 'become king' (14.9), establishing manifest power over all. Most specifically it is prophesied that the nations will flock to Jerusalem to worship him as king in the autumn festival (14.16).

Then the 'holiness' radiating from the Presence of God will shine into all life, so that not only the special priestly things, but all common life will be holy, having the quality to be in his presence, able to bear his nearness. Even the horses, so often deprecated for their foreign and military associations, will wear bells inscribed 'Holy to the Lord' (14.20), the very same inscription which the high priests wore when approaching the dread Presence on the Day of Atonement (Ex. 28.36).

Then too the water of life will flow constantly to east and west from the temple-city (Zech. 14.8). The order of night and day, light and dark, will give way to the steady light of the divine Presence. This indeed is a vision of God come forth from his hiddenness, a time when all that now seems essential in the cosmic order gives way to his Presence, the sole power able to shape a new world.

Jonah – an ironic tale

Among the books of the twelve 'minor' prophets, between Obadiah and Micah, we meet the Book of Jonah. But its character is quite different from that of the prophetic books, and we shall therefore only note it briefly. The historical prophet Jonah ('Dove') appears in II Kings 14.25. It is reported there how in the eighth century Jonah predicted that the king of Israel would regain some lost territory. But our Book of Jonah is a picturesque tale written about four centuries later, as its language shows.

The theological point of the tale is of great significance, showing that God's love is infinitely broader and deeper than the resentful, sectarian, nationalistic attitudes that warp many ostensibly pious people. The method of the writer is equally remarkable. Like Jesus, he creates a tale full of irony and humour to break through the hardened heart, and he ends with a question, leaving us to respond.

On the threshold of response

In a light presentation of the Book of Jonah (one of forty expositions in my *Interpreted By Love*, pp.138–142), I concluded as follows:

Of all the marvels (the writer of Jonah) relates, none, not even the swallowing of Jonah, is as miraculous as the perfect repentance of Nineveh. But he stops short of telling a final miracle, the changing of Jonah's heart. He ends with a question. He does so in case Jonah's heart is in some way our heart. In some way are we also more severe than God, begrudging forgiveness which he would extend? . . . Yes, the story ends with a question, only on the threshold of the greatest miracle, which will happen when another unloving barrier in our heart gives way to the persevering compassion of God.

For discussion or writing

– What different kinds of prophetic activity are illustrated by the books of Obadiah, Joel and Zechariah.

– It has been said that Obadiah, Joel and Zechariah show a remarkable ability to see the ultimate through the local. What illustrations can you give of this ability?

– What examples of irony can you find in the tale of Jonah?

WORDS FROM DANIEL

May the name of God be blessed from age to age
for to him belong wisdom and power!
He rules the changes of times and seasons,
deposing kings, installing kings,
giving to the wise their wisdom
and to the discerning their knowledge (2.20–21).

Then King Nebuchadnezzar was astonished and rose up in alarm, and said to his counsellors, Was it not three men that we threw bound into the fire? They answered the king, That is true, O king. He replied, But I see four men loose and walking about in the fire unharmed, and the appearance of the fourth is like a son of the gods (3.24–25).

They drank wine and praised the gods of gold, silver and bronze, iron, wood and stone. And suddenly there appeared the fingers of a human hand and wrote on the plaster of the wall . . . and the king changed colour; he was filled with alarm, his limbs gave way and his knees knocked together (5.4–5).

And as I am looking still in the visions of the night, see, with clouds of heaven comes one like a son of man and draws near to the Ancient of Days, and is presented before him. And to him is given sovereignty, glory and kingship, that all peoples, nations and languages shall serve him . . . an eternal sovereignty which will never pass away (7.13–14).

And many of those sleeping in earth's dust will awake,
some to everlasting life,
and some to shame and everlasting contempt.
And the wise will shine like the brightness of the firmament,
and those who make many right with God
like the stars for ever and ever (12.2–3.)

15

Daniel – Visions of the New Age

Clarifying terms

We have seen that the idea of a great intervention by God to judge and rectify the world was well-rooted in Israel and in the succession of great prophets. And we have seen that such expectations were strongly felt and expressed around the sixth and fifth centuries – so Joel, Obadiah, Haggai, Zechariah, Third Isaiah, Malachi, and we could add Isaiah 24–27.

To such expectations the term 'eschatology' is sometimes applied, meaning thought about the End-time. Another expression used is 'Apocalyptic', meaning revelation of final mysteries. But the material we have just mentioned is most conveniently described as 'early Apocalyptic'. When we move on a few centuries we meet expectations of the end which have a rather different character, and it is these that are best described simply as 'Apocalyptic'.

Apocalyptic books in the Greek and Roman eras

Alexander the Great swiftly conquered the Persian empire around 333 BCE. When he died in 323, his generals inherited the empire in two main portions and continued his very influential cultural policies. Greeks set the fashion for the key cities of the Near East. Their intellectual achievements mingled with the old oriental learning and religions, resulting in a lively mixed culture we call 'Hellenistic'.

Times were different also now within Jewry. A large body of scripture had been assembled and become respected, and the nation found its guides in men who were expert in scripture and learning. Sects with rival interpretations grew up. Prophets had ceased to be prominent nationally. But prophecy in scripture was keenly studied and related to present circumstances.

In time of crisis, encouraging books were written, full of a new form of 'Apocalyptic'. The learned authors often presented their message as if it were a long-range prediction made by a saint of far-off times, even from the beginning of mankind (Adam, Enoch, Lamech etc.). History was schematized into eras of empire, the next one due being the final, fulfilling kingdom of God. We meet elaborate symbols, numerology, dreams, and orders of angels. About twenty such works are known, some only in fragments.

Apocalyptic vision ascribed to Ezra

Examples of apocalyptic writing can be conveniently found in Bibles which contain the Apocrypha (meaning 'hidden' books, of disputed origin) – books preserved in the Greek, but not the Hebrew, Bible. From the work commonly cited as II Esdras (13.1–3) we have this vision ascribed to Ezra:

After seven days I dreamed a dream by night, and behold, there arose a wind from the sea, that stirred up all its waves. And I saw, and behold, this wind caused to come up from the midst of the sea as it were the likeness of a man, and I saw, and behold, that man flew with the clouds of heaven, and when he turned his face to look, all things trembled that were seen under him.

The setting of the Book of Daniel

The greatest crisis for Jewish religion came in the second century, particularly 167–164 BCE. The Holy Land was then in the empire of Antiochus IV, whose base was in Syria. He attacked the more conservative Jews and had the temple used in the style of Hellenistic religion. The Books of Maccabees (in the Apocrypha) give accounts of the sufferings of the persecuted groups.

The Book of Daniel seems to have been written in this situation. With a blend of stirring tales and apocalyptic visions, it aims to kindle the faith and courage of those under attack. Its message is that the crisis was foreknown and is within the sure purpose of God. The days of evil are numbered. Soon will come the kingdom of God, with joy for all the faithful, even for those who have died.

The contents of the Book of Daniel

The first part of the book consists chiefly of stories about faith and miracles set in the time of the Exile (as we judge, four centuries before the writer's time). In the second half the narrative introduces Daniel's visions, still set in the ancient period. They foretell the crisis of the writer's time (in effect the persecution under Antiochus IV) and predict a just and final outcome.

The writer's knowledge of the Babylonian period is in fact vague and confused. His hero Daniel may be an adaptation of a legendary Dan'el celebrated more widely in the ancient Near East (cf. Ezek. 14.14). We might compare the stories with the religious tales of the Books of Esther and (in the Apocrypha) Tobit and Judith; indeed the Greek Bible has more romances added to the Book of Daniel, telling of Susanna and the Elders, Bel and the Dragon, and the prophet Habakkuk's air-borne journey from Jerusalem to Babylon with a pot of stew for Daniel in the lion-pit.

The stories of Daniel, then, are creative writing. No doubt they draw on tradition, but their value is in their message, so memorably brought home. One kind tells of courage to take a stand, another tells of emperors suddenly punished, and a third explains history as a succession of empires about to be concluded with that of God. This last kind (so Dan. 2) covers also the stories of the visions in chs. 7–12. Curiously, 2.4–7.28 is not in Hebrew like the rest but in Aramaic. We may wonder if in dangerous times a damaged Hebrew manuscript had to be supplemented by its Aramaic translation.

In but not of the world

The stories of Daniel reflect a world where the Jews live and work in a Gentile culture. The heroes contribute much to the society, but take a stand when the fundamentals of their faith require it. Thus, chapter 3 tells of three young Jews who were happy to be educated in Babylonian wisdom and serve as administrators, but they preferred to be thrown into the fiery furnace, rather than bow down to the golden idol. The king is astonished to see them walking unharmed in the flames, and with them a fourth figure like a 'son of the gods', and he calls the three out and honours them.

In another vivid story with this theme (ch. 6) the main character is Daniel. Here again is an exiled Jew who has risen to eminence in Babylonian society as a sage and administrator. But again he comes to the limit, and refuses to give up his practice of kneeling in prayer three times a day in an upper window facing Jerusalem. He is consigned overnight to a den of lions, but comes out unharmed, to the joy of the king, who has fasted for him all night.

These stories illustrated God's faithfulness and power, without creating a dogma of deliverance. The three men threatened with the furnace believed in God's power to deliver them, but were content with his freedom to decide (3.18).

The second kind of story, about great rulers suddenly cast down, is not concerned with their foreignness, but with the question of arrogance and humility before heaven. Nebuchadnezzar, as Daniel has foretold by interpreting the king's dream, loses his reason and lives in the wild, but then learns humility under God and is restored (ch. 4). The doom of another overweening ruler, Belshazzar, is related in chapter 5. Here Daniel interprets the writing of a ghostly hand upon the wall, and that very night his interpretation is confirmed by events – the king is slain and Darius the Mede takes over the kingdom.

The approach of the everlasting kingdom

The third line of encouragement comes in materials which teach that, however evil the present regime, it is about to be swallowed up by God's perfect and predestined kingdom. The sufferers under Antiochus IV receive this message from stories of the ancient predictions of Daniel. They learn that a succession of four world empires was predestined, and they will recognize that the last one is in fact their own oppressor. So they are strengthened by the knowledge that the days of the evil empire are numbered, and that the time of the perfect kingdom, the kingdom of God, is at hand.

Visions ascribed to Enoch

One of the ancient figures said by the apocalyptic writers to have had visions of the end was Enoch. In Gen. 5.18–24 he appears in the seventh generation of the human race and as the father of the longest-lived of all, Methuselah. Enoch is especially notable as in Genesis it is not said that he died, but that, having walked with God, he was taken up (to heaven). In this extract from the Book of Enoch (37–39) we hear of the intercessions of the departed:

The second vision, the vision of wisdom, which Enoch saw . . . And I saw the dwellings of the holy ones and the places where the righteous rest. And they made request and interceded and prayed for the children of men. And righteousness flowed like water before them, and mercy like dew on the ground.

In accordance with this message, Daniel explains the king's dream of an image with head of gold, breast of silver, belly of bronze, and legs of iron (Dan. 2). These parts of the image signify the various world empires destined to succeed each other. The people of the author's time would think how the Babylonians had been succeeded by the Medes, the Persians, and now the Greeks, one of whom, Antiochus, was ruling with truly iron force. And gladly would they hear that soon the stone of God would strike the image's feet, that were mixed with clay. Then the monstrous image would crumble, and be whirled away by the wind, and on the messianic stone would be established the kingdom of God.

The same message emerges from the story of Daniel's own vision in chapter 7. Four beasts from the chaos-sea represent the succession of world empires. The many horns of the fourth beast represent particular kings of the Hellenistic empire. The last of these to sprout up, with eyes and bragging mouth, no doubt signifies Antiochus. But the court that sits in heaven before the Most High, the Ancient of Days, gives judgment against the fourth beast, which is duly slain. To whom will the kingdom now be given? Daniel recounts:

> And behold, with the clouds of heaven
>   came one like a son of man,
> and he came to the Ancient of Days
>   and was presented before him.
>
> And to him was given dominion . . .
>   that all peoples, nations and languages should serve him.
> His dominion is an everlasting dominion . . .
>   that shall not be destroyed.

The figure's man-like form contrasts with the monsters of chaos. Here is to be a just rule according to God's will. The figure represents the cause of 'the people of the holy ones of the Most High', but otherwise is not explained. In his exaltation God's faithful people receive the everlasting kingdom.

More visions of Enoch

The book of Enoch is of special interest because of passages concerning 'the Son of Man'. Here is an example (from 46.1–3):

And I saw One there who had an aged head, for it was white like wool, and with him was another with an appearance like that of a man, and his face was full of grace like that of a holy angel . . . And the angel said to me, This is the Son of Man with whom righteousness dwells, and who will reveal all the treasures of the hidden things.

Winning meaning out of death

Our author lived in a time when many had already been martyred for their faith. Hebrew religion had always been reluctant to speak of any worthwhile life after death for individuals. But now our author was moved to make what is in fact the clearest statement of life after death in the Hebrew Bible: 'Many of those who sleep in the dust of the earth shall awake, some to everlasting life, and some to shame and everlasting contempt' (12.2).

This is not a comprehensive statement about life after death. The context is the final deliverance of the people after the intervention of their guardian angel, Michael, in an unparalleled time of trouble. Of those who die before the final deliverance 'many', it is said, will rise again from the dust. In mind will have been the martyrs, now to be rewarded in everlasting life, and the persecutors, now to be punished in everlasting contempt. In 12.3 there are important echoes (not always obvious in our English translations) of the fourth Servant Song (Isa. 52.13–53.12). Those who have suffered patiently for God's sake are, like the Servant, 'triumphant' (*maskilim*, cf. Isa. 52.13), having 'made right the multitudes' (cf. Isa. 53.11). Thus the faithful sufferers have fallen in with the destiny of the Servant; his work of sacrifice, redeeming the many, has been seen in them.

Nearing the time of Jesus

Daniel is not presented as a prophet like those we have been studying. He is learned in books, expert in government, skilled in the interpretation of dreams. He is given enigmatic visions of detailed events in the remote future.

Nor is the Book of Daniel like the books of the prophetic collection. Half consists of gripping stories and half of enigmatic visions and revelations for a time still to come. It is our first example of the truly apocalyptic literature, and it is taking us much nearer to the faith-world of the New Testament. Although our English Bibles place Daniel between Ezekiel and Hosea, the Hebrew Bible, more appropriately, does not have it among the

Prophets, but towards the end of its last section, the Writings, miscellaneous books mostly of late date.

The Book of Daniel's chief resemblance to the religion of New Testament times is its expectancy for the kingdom of God, the everlasting age that will supercede the present world empire. Such expectancy was to grow ever stronger towards the time of Jesus. The old prophets and psalmists came to be read with one major question in mind: when would the ages be fulfilled, salvation and justice triumph for the living and the dead, and God's everlasting kingdom be established through his Chosen One?

For discussion or writing

– Highlight the differences between the prophetic and the apocalyptic literature through comparison of the books of Amos and Daniel.

– Write a poem incorporating the main points of Daniel 7.

– Imagine how the Book of Daniel might speak to someone in the midst of the suffering caused by one of the modern tyrannies.

16

Retrospect and Ruminations

Long ago God spoke in many and various ways to the
ancestors through the prophets (Heb. 1.1).

The setting for our subject was the ancient Near East. Just as the
Hebrew language was rooted in that wide environment, and had
much in common with neighbouring languages, and yet came to
have its own character and make its own contribution, so the
practice of Hebrew prophecy was widely rooted across many
frontiers, yet grew to have a peculiar significance.

Those ancient peoples shared a lively sense of heaven's concern
with their affairs. Nations with their wars and economies,
individuals with their births, health and deaths – all was seen as
governed by the divine power. Not surprisingly, we found that
there was a profusion of kinds of intermediaries, people who
could pass on knowledge of the divine intentions or work for
their modification. Some served at great religious centres, some in
humbler localities. Women or men, these intermediaries might
serve full-time or only occasionally. Some were highly regulated
and likely to use technical methods. Others less predictably
gained their knowledge in trances or visions, appearing as
messengers of heaven, commissioned perhaps in the divine
council – such were the prophetic souls. But while the range of
mediating work gave rise to varieties of mediators and methods,
there was a degree of fluidity between them. An intimate of
heaven could appear in more than one role.

We found that among the Israelites the range of intermediaries
was indicated by quite a variety of names covering the roles of

priests, diviners, healers, seers, ascetics, the wise, Gods's intimates, his spokespersons. The main term usually rendered 'prophet' was *nabi* ('prophetess' *nbi'a*), probably meaning '(God's) spokesperson'. But here again were signs of fluidity, with some prophets on occasion acting like priests and others having certainly come from one of the classes of priest.

Our knowledge of the practice of prophecy in the neighbouring countries is growing steadily, though it is as yet rather fragmentary. Already it seems likely that any Syrian, Moabite, Babylonian or Assyrian trader visiting the Hebrew people would not have found the general activities of their prophets at all surprising. Yet through the many Hebrew link-persons down the ages, some impressive, some we think less so, some touching the lives of kings and nations, some known only in small communities, a weighty tradition begins to take shape.

Biblical chroniclers of the past, with a blend of history and legend, tell of great figures such as Moses, Samuel, Nathan, Elijah and Elisha. But the prophetic books of the Bible, from Isaiah to Malachi, the objects of our study, give us something astonishing and certainly unique. For here in profusion are the actual sayings and poems of a succession of prophets, men who saw deeply into the condition and destiny of their people during several centuries of crisis and tragedy.

We came to see how in their criticisms of morality and religion they embraced the whole of life. They saw a doom that must fall on the corrupt society. But they also saw the Creator as persevering in his good purpose for that people and for all creation. The original powerful words were passed down through a succession of disciples and other preservers of tradition. Other materials might be gathered to them, till the whole came to be edited in the books we now have, forming a unique tapestry of condemnation and hope, a world's doom and rebirth.

By his faithfulness he gained recognition as a prophet,
and by his words he was known to be a trustworthy seer
(Ecclus. 46.15).

When we thought of the ministries behind the prophetic

books, it did not seem necessary to picture a new type of ministry, a new kind of prophet. At the great pilgrimage festivals of the royal states of Israel and Judah there had developed, it seems, a tradition of expressing God's word to the nation, and even to the nations. To the faith of the pilgrims it was a logical sequence: the coming of the Lord into the midst of the gathering led on to prophetic mediation of his assessment of the nation and his decree for their destiny (as can be seen from Ps. 50, 81, 95). There was an opportunity here for the development of prophetic speeches directed to a vast audience, dealing with great matters of the nation and the world, radical in criticism, immense in hope.

In relation to such a tradition we can best understand the prophets of the prophetic books, most of whom clearly worked in or around the great sanctuary. On occasion they have a word or action for an individual king or commoner. But it seems that it was for their pronouncements about the nation that they were distinguished, weighty words bearing on extreme crises, words that were vindicated by later events. Thus it was that their followers felt bound to preserve and develop their words towards the present written form. When all might have seemed lost, their words gave direction and hope.

Prophecy on this scale accompanied the last two centuries of Hebrew monarchy, culminating in the Babylonian Exile, and survived a little longer into the Persian period. The old prophetic words gradually became part of a great body of scripture, and the existence of this scripture was now a factor in the fading away of this kind of prophetic activity. Leadership fell rather to experts in the scriptural law. Without a king, furthermore, the nation had less scope for political decision, and the festal assemblies had less political significance. From such factors, it seems, it came about that there was never again to be a prophet like Amos, Isaiah and the others.

Courageous, profound, timely – such were their words to an extraordinary degree. But we found that we should beware of assuming that they were innovative. Their insights had parallels in earlier centuries. But in application of received truth, and in the total effect of their words and ministries, they are truly outstanding, virtually unique.

> *My doctrine shall drop as the rain*
> *and my speech distil as the dew,*
> *as the small rain falls on the tender grass*
> *and as showers upon the herb* (Deut.32.2).

That our prophets were much more than messengers is obvious when we consider the poetic nature of their utterance. We saw that for most of them the natural vehicle of prophecy was a poetry allied to chant or music, a poetry powerful in rhythm, in patterns of parallelism, imagery and sound play; not a poetry crafted with labour of mind and pen, but a poetry that could spring from a reservoir of ancient forms and phrases and flow immediately from the prophet's heart and mouth.

It is easy to see the fitness of poetic speech and chant for the realm of oral teaching. Not only the memory but also the imagination is better served by the beautiful language, its balance, melody and dance.

But more significant was the link of this prophetic poetry with the poetry of the Psalms, and so with the worship that was at home in the temple. It is striking that our prophets and the Psalms both share the elements, of poetic prayer, praise, and oracle. The difference is in the proportion of these elements, with the oracles (first person speech of God) preponderating in the prophets. Even so, the closeness of the poetry of the prophets to that of the Psalms shows how this prophetic tradition was rooted in worship, especially those occasions in the temple where vision, poetry and music had their great opportunity.

But if the poetry of our prophets points us to the needs of oral teaching and worship, still more it tells us of the intensity of their inspiration. They were visionary souls, with focussed mind and heightened powers of listening and speaking. In such a case ideas burn brightly and words begin to dance. The language is lifted by the pulse of the dance and the passion of music. Prophecy and poetry become one.

All these aspects of the prophetic poetry help us to see why these prophets are still so fruitful today. In moral and religious teaching, in preaching and spiritual study, the colour and beauty of their poetry still feed the imagination and impress the memory. In worship their poetry resounds continually: be it Christmas, Holy Week, harvest, or an occasion of great social concern, their poetry draws the worshippers strongly into the divine world. And finally, the poetic nature of our prophets reveals their bond with the true poets of our times, indeed with all creative souls who have risked their lives and sanity in exposing themselves to truth. With the supremely brave and sensitive poets and artists of all ages, our Hebrew prophets have a bond.

> *Thus says the Lord:*
> *Stand by the ways*
> *and look and ask for the ancient paths,*
> *for the way of goodness,*
> *and walk in it*
> *and find rest for your souls* (Jer. 6.16).

We found that while our prophets were not pioneers of the belief that there was only one true, full God, they were outstanding in showing what his sovereignty must mean for human society. Lively realization of what was due to him was liable to be dulled. The prophets saw how people could in practice cease to 'know' him – through their reliance on human strength, through greed, ambition, callousness, or through the lure of fertility cults. No new theory of God and his oneness was needed, but rather hearts awakened to his holiness and glory, knowing his awesome divine being as the factor of overwhelming importance in all circumstances of life. Towards the end of this prophetic era, the ancient perception embodied in the very name of the Lord, 'Yahweh', was most fully spelt out and declared by a successor of Isaiah: The Lord is He who Is, and Only Is, centre and source of reality, Creator and King of all, who will not allow any to usurp his sovereignty. The lives of our prophets were filled with awareness of this God and served greatly to foster such awareness in others.

Their special sensitivity was to his working in the current national and international circumstances. They inherited the faith that this Lord of all the world had chosen to centre his work in a specially called and guided people. This people so blessed were all the more responsible, and our prophets felt driven to make terrible indictments. Their targets were all kinds of abuses arising from greed and arrogance, especially social injustice and infidelity to the bond with the Lord. They saw on every hand a lack of 'knowledge of God', which meant primarily a lack of living relationship with him. Sin was violation of such relationship, repentance was a returning to him, a seeking, finding, and resting in him.

But as our prophets looked deeply into the hearts of the people, especially those devoted to the possession of wealth and power, they saw little hope of such returning. Yet they did not finally yield to despair, to barren cynicism or hatred of mankind. They had hope, an assurance of all at last made well, and it rested solely on perception of the grace of God. The attributes of God all pointed to the ultimate victory of his good purpose – his holiness, righteousness, compassion, faithfulness, and above all his *ḥesed*, his committed, enduring, persevering love.

We saw that questions might be raised about the tendency in prophetic thinking to view a whole people as one corporate personality. They might see their own people as a young woman fallen dead to the ground, or as the Lord's unfaithful wife, or as his headstrong son. The ancestor Jacob still lived through the life of the people; all collectively represented him, were virtually identical with him and could be addressed by the Lord as 'Jacob my servant'. Not only was a people seen as one person, but this person transcended the generations through the centuries. A generation centuries after the Exodus could be told, 'I brought you up out of the land of Egypt.'

On the positive side, this collective way of thinking emphasized the mutual responsibility of individuals in a shared life. If one limb suffered, the whole body was distressed, as St Paul was later to put it. The collective view also enabled the prophets to present the bond of God and people in terms of intimate love – the husband and wife, the parent and child.

On the negative side, there were problems of justice to individuals and of giving due weight to individual responsibility. It might be a fact that sometimes when a generation ate sour grapes, it was the teeth of the next generation that were set on edge (Ezek. 18.2–4), but was it just?

The collective view could therefore not stand alone. While it could still be usefully preserved, alongside it must be recognition of individual responsibility. And so in our prophets we find that alongside characteristic denunciations of a whole people are statements of a discriminating judgment. The avenging Lord might hold a sieve to sift out sinners, or an inkhorn to mark with a cross the brows of those to be spared, or a book recording the names of those who had shown reverence. In the dreadful day, the humble might be sheltered, a remnant spared.

Oracles announcing a comprehensive and complete salvation make a stark contrast with the words of doom and are treated by some modern critics as additions of a later age. Some may be so, but a substantial number should be judged as clearly rooted in the ministry of the great prophets. It is wise to recognize that the concepts of divine judgment used by our prophets had in their essence a positive purpose, requiring in the end a positive outcome.

At some times and to some audiences a prophet might feel bound to present the negative side only. He still did so persuasively, and it can be inferred that he had not finally abandoned all hope of repentance. The main concepts used were those of the covenant and of God's kingship. With the covenant there could be hope of a fresh beginning beyond discipline, while the theology of God as king spoke of his purging the world of corruption, but also of putting right the lives of the oppressed. From the visions born in the deep experiences of dramatic festal worship, when something of the perfected kingdom seemed already to shine on the worshippers, our prophets could draw, when appropriate, to speak of ultimate salvation.

> *The Lord God has spoken.*
> *who can but prophesy?* (Amos 3.8).

One may imagine it was after a difficult birth or for a very frail baby that the name 'Amos' was given, signifying 'The Lord has carried this child'; only a carrying by the Lord himself could have saved, and now saves, this new life. In such a case parents would often dedicate the growing child to the service of the temple; it is interesting that the commander who bore the full form of the name, Amasiah, is expressly described as 'dedicated freely to the Lord' (II Chron. 17.16). At all events, we saw that there is reason to think that the sheep-masters of Tekoa, among whom Amos was reckoned, may have looked after flocks, herds and trees belonging to the Jerusalem temple.

Tekoa was a fortified city eleven miles south of Jerusalem, and it was thither that David's army chief had sent when he needed the services of a 'wise woman' (II Sam. 14). The woman is never named, and the wording suggests that Joab sent to a renowned institution or circle able to supply such a skilled woman, rather than just to a famous individual. The city, then, may have been a place having links with the personnel of the Jerusalem sanctuary, and boasting a circle of 'wise' persons, having psychic gifts and knowledge.

Not himself a nabi, nor the disciple of a nabi, Amos worked with cattle and the cultivation of sycamore figs (nipping the fruit for ripening) until one day the call came: 'The Lord took me from behind the flock and the Lord said to me, Go, serve as a nabi to my people Israel.' (The Hebrew verb usually translated here 'prophesy' is developed from the noun 'nabi', and means 'act as nabi'.)

Whether Amos was able without more ado to undertake his journeys to the shrines of Israel and Judah and speak with such mastery of the tradition of poetical prophecy and with such wisdom and knowledge, or whether he first attached himself to masters in these things, we are not told. But his speeches seem to be examples of a tradition matured over centuries, a poetic tradition which ten or twenty years later was represented even more splendidly by Isaiah and Micah. The chief priest at Bethel, Amaziah, knew Amos, in the climax of his ministry, as a Judean *ḥozeh* (seer, visionary prophet) and felt that the very earth was quaking at his words.

The main target of Amos was the northern kingdom, and

Amaziah thought he would do better to go off and direct his fire against his native Judah. Jerusalem, Judah and Beersheba are mentioned in the denunciations, but almost in passing, and it is the northern capital Samaria and its great shrines Bethel and Gilgal which bear the brunt of the condemnation. One may wonder if the duties of his first employment had taken Amos often into the northern kingdom. That kingdom in any case had probably gone further than Judah down the road of ruthless commercialism, being more open to the great commercial centres and routes of the Near Eastern and Mediterranean world. There it was that he saw 'the breaking of Joseph', the dispossession and enslavement of the humbler folk. There it was that he saw with divine fury the assembling in the house of God of those who profited from such hard-hearted injustice. And there it was that he delivered his most telling denunciations and predictions of doom.

With all the eloquence of a great poet he sought to convince, and one must feel that some hope still drove him, hope which seemed indeed to shine out when he called for the justice of compassion to roll through the nation like the waters of a mighty perennial stream, or when he cried 'Seek the Lord and live!' True, he came to see that the state dominated by the royal family and the wealthy classes must be shattered, though he had made repeated intercessions for 'Jacob'. But he must surely have believed that the Lord would save the oppressed and at last establish a just realm. And so we conclude that the positive end of the book, which has links with the beginning, can at least be taken to represent his underlying faith.

There is no truth or faithful love
or knowledge of God in the land (Hos. 4.1).

The strange circumstances of Hosea's marriage dominate the beginning of the book, but not for biographical interest. Whatever the character of his wife Gomer and her subsequent history, the incidents are placed prominently because of what they signify for others. Hosea married her to signify that his people were unfaithful to God. Continuing his symbolic action, he named their subsequent children to signify judgment and estrangement for his people. Then, in a manner not quite clear to us, he went again to love and redeem, to signify the Lord's purpose to bring his people through discipline back to mutual love. And further to this, it seems that the children's names were reversed in meaning, to signify the Lord's taking his people in compassion back to himself.

In spite of not answering all our questions, this material gives us essential information about the message of this prophet of the northern kingdom. We saw that he had to work in the growing disorder of the kingdom as the Assyrians gradually destroyed it. His words were narrowly rescued for posterity by being some-how brought to Judah. The hazards have had their effect on the clarity of the book. But through the precious record we discern a passionate and sensitive prophet, who saw the evil in his society and declared the doom and estrangement that would ensue, but who came to know also, as it were, the colossal struggle of judgment and compassion in the heart of God, and the invincible nature of the divine love: 'How can I give you up, how hand you over? My heart is overturned within me, all my compassion is kindled, I will not execute my anger, for I am God not man, the Holy One in your midst.'

Hosea nevertheless foresaw that destruction must come and that this people, this child of God, must know again the nakedness of life in the desert. Its political, social and religious worlds must collapse, before the tender call of God could be heard again, the grace of the Lord come as the dew, and the beloved blossom as the lily.

> *But as for me, I will look to the Lord,*
> *I will wait for the God of my salvation.*
> *Though I fall, I shall arise.*
> *When I dwell in darkness*
> *the Lord shall be a light to me* (Micah 7.7–5).

At the birth of Micah, gratitude, love and awe must have welled up in the hearts of his parents, for they made him all his life a testimony by naming him 'Who is like Yahweh?' In due course he came up from the little fortress-town in the south to serve the

Lord in Jerusalem. There he may have fallen under the influence of the outstanding prophet Isaiah, but he was to be remembered as himself a powerful prophet. No one spoke stronger words than he against the exploitation of the poor and the devious motives of princes, priests and prophets. He warned of judgment that would fall on the two capital cities – fine palaces to be thrown down the hill-sides, the very soil of the holy city ploughed as a field. And we noted that in Jerusalem his words bore some fruit, and the king led acts of penitence.

Positive sides, however, were not lacking in Micah's preaching. He spelt out the Lord's requirements: not spectacular ritual offerings, but what the heart had always known when it was quiet and true – the doing of justice, the loving of kindness, and a humble walking with God.

We found that on other occasions at the assemblies for worship he would lead prayers in the poetic, singing style of the psalms. He would lament to the Lord for the dearth of trustworthy people, and for the violence and corruption that spoiled family life. It was not the lament of helpless despair, and he was able to turn to the people again with a message of good beyond the time of suffering. Echoing his name, he would conclude with a song of thanksgiving: 'Who is a god like you? You will cast all their sins into the depths of the sea. You will deal faithfully with Jacob.'

Like his contemporary, Isaiah, he had creative words for the royal line. As through swirls of mist, we discern from his words the outline of a suffering king, and then from little Bethlehem a light of eternal salvation, God's true shepherd. In another striking prophecy, his own or one he was glad to adopt, he sees the humble hill of the temple raised high above all other mountains. It is a vision of a world where communion with God is paramount for all nations, and justice and peace prevail.

What do you mean by crushing my people,
and by grinding the faces of the poor? (Isa. 3.15).

We are shown the prophet Isaiah in a variety of scenes. As a young man, he stands in the nave of the Jerusalem temple during the ceremonies connected with the autumnal new year. The glory of the Lord's newly-proclaimed reign is revealed to him with an actuality beyond ordinary senses. He sees the Holy One in all his majesty, with throne, robes, heavenly attendants and council, and he becomes the envoy of the Lord's decree for the fate of the assembled people.

It is likely that he again takes part in the autumnal worship when he provides the song for the divine bridegroom who has come to his bride Zion. He sings of the Lord's love for his beautiful 'vineyard', and of his shock to find, not sweet grapes, but sour. With punning Hebrew words, the prophet sings of the justice and compassion that God looked for, and the cruelty and crying that he found.

Perhaps also it was at the same pilgrimage season, so rich in opportunity for prophets, that Isaiah was able to tell of prospects beyond the havoc, when the dynasty of David and the holy mountain would be truly instruments of God's perfected kingdom.

Out and about we see Isaiah with messages for kings, and sometimes entering the palace, which adjoined the temple. By the water that flowed quietly from the spring to the royal gardens he gave counsel in the face of invasion; there he spoke of calm trust and the mysterious salvation that was hidden up for the dynasty. And somewhere in public he walked 'naked and barefoot' over a period of three years. It was a sign in another international crisis, a predictive parable of prisoners led away after Assyrian conquest.

Several vivid scenes are preserved in Isa. 36–39, which, if partly of legendary character, can still show us aspects of his ministry. To the elderly prophet, Hezekiah sent his senior ministers and priests to seek a word from the Lord in a desperate time, a time when children come to the birth but there is no strength to bring them forth (Isa. 37). But when Hezekiah was ill, Isaiah went to the palace to warn of death, then, returning, to announce a reprieve and to prescribe a remedy (Isa. 38).

He was no less outraged by social oppression than was Amos, only now the focus was on Jerusalem and Judah. He too used a brilliant poetic eloquence to denounce abuses of the judicial system against vulnerable people, and to announce retribution from the Lord, yet still with an appeal (1.16–20).

On several occasions Isaiah is shown intervening in the policies of state. In times of peril from aggressive powers, his character-istic message was neither jingoistic prediction of victory nor plain prediction of defeat. With the survival of the nation in the balance, with the din of warfare approaching, he would speak to kings and statesmen of quiet trust, firm faith, and the marvellous purposes of God above all human pretensions (7.9; 30.15). He poured scorn on trust in coalitions of states, perceiving their unreliability with a penetrating realism.

No politician, balancing pressures, fixing up the short term, could ever have found him an easy counsellor to follow. He was aware of the majesty of the Lord (2.10–22; 5.15–16; 6.3; 18.4) as few are, and he drew consequences as few will do.

For those who scoffed at 'the purposes of the Holy One' (5.19) he had withering words. He saw clearly an evil which we may think also characterizes our own society, with its culture of slick and deceptive advertising, promoted by the most wealthy, executed by the most talented – the sin of calling evil good and good evil, of putting darkness for light and bitter for sweet (5.20). And still not uncommon today are those he castigated as 'wise in their own eyes, shrewd in their own sight', and those valiant when it comes to drinking or taking bribes (5.21–23).

Of all the prophecies of messianic times, none can surpass those of Isa. 2, 9 and 11. What wonder, after all these years, still arises at the Child that is born, the Son that is given, whose name shall be Wonderful Counsellor, Prince of Peace! What joy at the vision of the Spirit-blessed king who will bring the rule of good-ness, when the animals will share the friendship and peace and none shall harm, and the knowledge of the Lord will rest deep over all the earth as the waters cover the sea!

The visions are all the more wonderful in that we meet them alongside Isaiah's portrayals of the evil in his society and the doom it must bring. The hinge between the two scenarios, doom and bliss, was an anticipatory experience of God's full reign. This experience was rooted in the celebration of God's kingship in the autumn festival and can be traced in the Psalms. For Isaiah it became a burning reality, dominating all his outlook. And so it could be that, as sure as he was that God the King would sweep away all that was corrupt and cruel, so sure he was no less that God would establish his kingdom in joyful peace, a kingdom mediated by a branch from the tree of Jesse and by the holy hill of Zion.

We are fortunate that so much was preserved from the years of Isaiah's ministry. But the book, in the light of modern scholarship, reveals also that his work continued to bear fruit and his influence to continue through later generations. It seems that he was able to form a prophetic circle, perhaps including his 'prophetess' wife and his symbolically named sons, a circle that could draw in new generations of prophetic apprentices and long continue. He relates, not the founding of the circle, but the role it was given. Guarding in their hearts and in their midst his holy teachings, and remaining available to the people coming to the sanctuary, they are to meet every request for divination or guidance by recourse to his 'teaching and testimony'. Through times of deep darkness these disciples, these 'children', are to be guardians and witnesses of all that the Lord has shown Isaiah, pointing the way to the time of fulfilment when the great light will arise. Not as an organization in itself would the circle be able to endure, but as a continuance of Isaiah's own 'waiting' and 'hoping' in the Lord (8.16–20):

> Now that I have bound the testimony
>   and sealed the oracles in my disciples,
> I wait for the Lord
>   who has hidden his face from the house of Jacob
>   and I look to him in hope.
> Behold, I and the children the Lord has given me
>   are signs and portents in Israel from the Lord of Hosts
>   who abides on Mount Zion.
> And when they say to you,
>   Consult for us the spirits . . .
> then to (my) teaching and testimony!

And we were to see that the faithful waiting was sustained, through several generations and the darkness of exile, until there sounded from this circle again a message of comfort and glory.

> *Seek righteousness, seek humility,*
> *and perhaps you will find shelter*
> *on the day of the Lord's anger* (Zeph. 2.3).

With the power of the Assyrian empire passing its zenith, and a remarkable young king, Josiah, reigning in Jerusalem, there was fresh need to read the signs of the times. Interpretations given by three prophets have been preserved in small books, each of three chapters, and each with a highly significant arrangement.

Indeed, we found that Zephaniah unfolds like a drama, a three-act presentation of the Day of the Lord. In the first act the prophet sets the sins of Jerusalem's leading citizens in a context of the end of the world, when an all-consuming divine fire of judgment will rage across the earth. Their evil deeds are the work of smug and callous hearts, and the prophet wants them to awake up to the reality of a judgment that is both terrible and hastening fast upon them.

In the second act, Zephaniah opens a little hope along the way of humility before God, but continues to depict judgment for the world and for the ravening wolves that he sees in the officials, judges, prophets and priests of Jerusalem, that rebellious, defiled, oppressing city – what an abode for the righteous God of the world!

A long silence would be needed for these fearsome words to sink in. But at last the final act is unfolded. Beginning quietly (3.9), the oracles depict the restoration of a pure world and its pure communion with the Lord. Peopled by the humble, the holy city is again at the centre, as beloved bride of God. Zephaniah, perhaps of royal and African descent, can envisage the Saviour's own delight expressed in the music and dance of love.

> *The violence done to (the forests of) Lebanon*
> *will overwhelm you,*
> *the destruction of the animals*
> *will terrify you* (Hab. 2.17).

With Habakkuk we saw more deeply into the work of the prophets as intercessors. In a poetry like that of the lamenting psalms he appeals to the Lord forcibly. There is a sharp edge to the prayers that contrast belief in God's goodness with the many years of cruel dominance he has allowed to the Assyrian empire. There is tenacious persistence in the repeated intercessions and the long vigils of waiting for an answer, like the vigil of a watchman on his tower. Waiting, ever waiting for the Lord – such is the lot of those who now suffer. But the word that comes from Habakkuk fills the waiting with a positive sense. The waiting becomes a confidence that, though the Lord's action seems slow, drawn out over long years, it will not be late. It comes at its right time, and the faithful waiting proves to be a conquering force.

The musical rubrics of Habakkuk 3 were added when the prayer-vision of that chapter was re-used and re-lived. But they follow naturally from the original inspiration, when the prophet prayed and depicted his vision of God in chanted poetry and psalmic style. With Habakkuk we see the unity of prayer, poetry, music, and prophecy.

He was named after a beautiful and beneficial herb. Hidden from us is the impulse for that naming, and we can only wonder about the disposition of his mother and her influence on him. But it is a fact that he is outstanding in the condemnation he heaps on those who have ravaged the great forests, destroyed the animals, and violated the earth itself. Many are his references to animals, and evident is his feeling for them. We may remember him in his faith, prayer and music as a spirit indeed like the doe he imagined leaping over the rugged mountains.

> *Woe to the bloody city,*
> *all full of lies and plunder!* (Nahum 3.1).

In Nahum we met a prophet whose poetic inspiration became a weapon. What has been preserved of his prophesying has one theme and one aim. Through his poetry he gives himself to become a weapon against Nineveh, the seat of the Assyrian emperor. In depicting the assault of divinely-stirred armies, then the assault and then the elegies, he feels he is used to bring about the judgment on that bastion of insatiable oppression. His poetry is like a powerful prayer, but, more than that, a prophetic act which traces out the reality to come, and brings it on.

So, in accordance with his name, he shows how 'God comforts' his people, and how the regular proclamation of God's kingdom in the festivals (when the feet of the tidings-bearer race over the mountains, 1.15) can take on reality in a historic upheaval. It is true that the material preserved contains no critique of Judah. But its message is not negligible, for it tells of God's sovereignty over earth's kingdoms, his invincible 'fury' against cruel arrogance, and his goodness to those who take refuge in him.

Woe to him who builds his palace with wrong-doing,
    and his high rooms with injustice,
who has people toil without payment
    and will not pay what they have earned!
Do you think you are a king
    because you can boast of your cedar-work?   (Jer. 22.13–16).

We found that to gain a fair impression of Jeremiah it was necessary to begin with an analysis of the large book that stands under his name. This highly sensitive, poetic prophet was in danger of being buried in a mass of sombre and repetitive prose not of his writing.

Yet when analysis into three main strands was made, their three-fold witness and the sheer abundance of material were able to inform us about this prophet with extraordinary fullness. So it has come about that as we follow the people's tragic descent, through half a century, to the bottom of the abyss, we can trace the ministry of the faithful prophet who never left them.

He was 'only a youth' when first called, and even six years later he was not yet the prophet that the good king Josiah would turn to. Rather it was the prophetess Huldah, no doubt a senior and renowned figure, who was consulted about the great reform (II Kings 22.14). But as the years went by, in spite of hostility that nearly destroyed him, he came to be the prophet that a worried government would consult. They valued him, even when they lacked the courage to heed him.

As a prophetic sign, he had no wife and children; he was living already in the bereavement that was to befall the nation. So neither did he sit in the company of merrymakers. He sat alone, because the Lord's hand was upon him. 'Why is my pain unceasing, and my wound uncurable?' he asked in his prayers. 'Will you be to me like a deceitful brook, like waters that fail?' In the answer he received there was reassurance, but also confirmation that he would ever bear the hostility of the people.

But fortunately there were some brave and loyal helpers, leading figures who hid him from King Jehoiaqim's anger, Baruch who assisted in his ministry, the Ethiopian who saved him from death in the cistern, and those who preserved his prophecies and signs.

And so it will always be possible for suffering poets and prophets to take courage from his example. Those who stay with their people in a tragic time will know something of the passions that were turned against him, and will not wonder at the emotion and violence of his prayers, but rather at his endurance, integrity and hope.

And all may wonder at the poetry that exposes the folly of a society that seems so like ours. He shows the horrible truth of prophets prophesying falsely, priests following them, and God's own people happy to have it so. He shows this people's double crime in forsaking the Lord, their fountain of living waters, and making for themselves in substitution cracked cisterns that soon run dry. It is a skilled society, but its skill is used for doing evil, and it no longer knows how to do good. Like well-fed stallions, the prosperous neigh for their neighbour's wife. Fat and sleek, the rich fill their great houses with the products of treachery; as fowlers trap birds in basketfuls, so they trap people. Yet they come to the temple as models of public virtue, making the holy place a den of robbers.

If only they had the sense of the birds that pass in their thousands through the land-corridor of Palestine according to the law their Maker has given them – stork, turtle-dove, swallow and crane! But alas, they bring a doom on all the earth, a desolation and a silence, when all the birds will have fled and mankind be no more seen, cities in ruins, mountains shaking, the skies darkened, and chaos returning. So the prophet sees.

But he knows it is not without God. If it were only a man-made ruin, there would indeed be no hope. But the anger of God is the judgment of the almighty and purposeful Creator, the divine Potter whose fingers shape, destroy, and make again. The time of compassion returns, the everlasting love is revealed. And so Jeremiah leaves words of hope ringing through the darkness: 'They shall come and sing on the height of Zion, their faces radiant at the goodness of the Lord. Their soul will be like a watered garden, with no more drooping. I will comfort them and give them gladness for sorrow. I will make a new covenant, writing my law on their hearts. I will forgive their wrongdoing and remember their sin no more' (31.12–13, 31–34).

> *Behold, you are to them like a singer of love-songs,*
> *with a beautiful voice and skilled on the strings;*
> *gladly they hear your words,*
> *but never do them* (Ezek. 33.32).

Ezekiel is careful to give us the year, the month, the day, the setting and the place, all in one sentence that ends by telling us that the heavens opened and he saw visions of God! Already in that first sentence we meet the striking combination of priestly detail and prophetic vision, the pedantry of the sacred lawyer and the ecstasy of the prophet, which is his hallmark. The sentence also gives us the key to his ministry as the breaking of light into the darkness of exile, the assurance of God's nearness in the valley of forsakenness. But above all, the sentence shows us what in his mind was the essential thing for all the hard service of his ministry. The heavens had opened to him, the glory of God had drawn near to him, and henceforward all that he was and did flowed from that experience. No wonder that this vision at his call is set out with extraordinary fullness and detail!

The whole book shares with this opening narrative the awe of the transcendent that is yet present. Ezekiel was from a line of priests that for centuries had been the chief priesthood at the

Jerusalem temple, and such a sanctuary was intended to mediate the Presence with every precaution to respect the aweful, transcendent mystery. And so it is that Ezekiel's accounts of the Lord's appearing and speaking to him are expressed in guarded style, full of circumlocution. There is always the sense that it is the Most High who addresses a mere mortal, a 'son of man'. And the divine actions are said to be motivated by God's will to vindicate the holiness of his great name.

But along with this austereness, this stiffness, this reserve, there is a powerful sense of God at work in his world. His hand is on the prophet, his Spirit is breathed into him. And the prophet's pastoral work, his daily work to the end of his life, is a reflection of the Lord's will himself to seek the lost sheep, bind up the injured and guard over the healthy.

With so many chapters predicting destructive judgment for Jerusalem and for various nations, the book makes heavy reading indeed, not lightened by its style. But our study revealed the importance of this brave prophet, who served and died in a period of tragedy. To this prophet, who was sometimes unable to speak, and whose utterances were often so ungracious, we owe some of the greatest images of faith in the transforming, saving grace of God. We best remember him for the miracles of the dry bones, the spring that healed the desert and the sea of death, the return of the Presence to the new Jerusalem, the living, tender hearts that replaced the hearts of stone, the divine Shepherd who saves his lost sheep.

Perhaps, after all, this is why the scroll packed with words of doom tasted sweet to Ezekiel – they were indeed divine words, and instinctively he knew that they were the beginning of a judgment that would end with the transformation to good. And this was the way that the Creator would reveal and finally assert the holiness of his great name.

The treasures of darkness will I give you,
and hordes from secret places (Isa. 45.13).

We came to see 'Second Isaiah' as a name of convenience for the prophetic voices we hear in Isaiah 40–55. It seemed likely that a highly gifted prophet led this outburst, while others of his circle also made contributions. The style, so different from that of Ezekiel (who was only a little earlier, and in the same region), was lyrical, psalm-like; and the themes and visions drew on memory of the great pilgrimage festivals of Jerusalem under the Davidic kings.

The flow of prophecy came as answer to the laments of a solemn assembly. That the occasion was a marking of the old holy days for the autumnal new year seemed likely from the content of the prophecies. Atonement, the processional advent of the Lord to Zion, the kingship of the Lord revealed in glory to the world, the vocation of the royal Servant, the renewal of Zion, the salvation of the outcast and poor, the dialogue of God and people, the sacred feast – such scenes from the festivals of old were now re-created in prophecy that related it all (rather as Nahum had done before the Exile) to a new era of history.

It might seem surprising that such a large and coherent body of prophecy, with its time, place and occasion of origin fairly obvious, should be anonymous. How was the name of so great and eloquent a prophet not handed down? It may have been because the main voice and the supporting voices in this cycle sounded from a group so dedicated to the tradition of Isaiah's prophecies that their own individuality was of no concern. If they belonged to later generations of the circle which Isaiah instituted to guard in their midst 'the teaching and testimony', their own inspirations, like those of earlier and later members, were grafted on to the living tradition without need being felt for a new authenticating name.

The cycle is unusually clear and coherent. Yet a particular problem of coherence troubles the thoughtful student. Where does the Suffering Servant fit in? If the prophets brought to the exiles a message of restoration through God-given victories of Cyrus the Persian, why did they include the presentation of the Servant, with its air of timeless, poetical mystery?

Within a great variety of scholarly opinions, there are interpretations which would diminish the importance of the Servant Songs for the message about the Lord's new kingdom. But it seemed more satisfactory to acknowledge the essential part of the Songs in the crescendo of the message, reaching the grand climax in chs. 52–53. And such acknowledgment became possible when the relation to the old festivals was given full weight. For the autumn festivals of royal Jerusalem had celebrated the ideal reign of God with reference to the ideal service required of the Davidic ruler. Our prophets' re-creation of the festival's world of ideas meant that they saw the forthcoming return from exile as the manifestation of the Lord's reign, involving the mediating work of his Servant, his royal Chosen One.

The rise of the Persian empire did not turn out to bring the full realization of the Lord's reign or the Servant's role. The prophets' vision transcended the meaning of the historical crisis. From the depths of ancient liturgy and the inspiration of a supreme poet-prophet, there has emerged a vision which illumines all history. It thus turns out to be appropriate that the prophecies do not clearly identify the Servant. Like the kingdom itself, he remains a mystery which can be experienced but not possessed.

It is interesting to see the struggle these prophets had with their people, as reflected especially in Isaiah 40–48. No doubt the hearers were wary of prophecies of imminent return, having been disappointed before. But they had also suffered from the loss of the spiritual joy of the festivals, those celebrations of the fresh coming of the Lord into their midst, making the temple a well of new life. The Isaiah prophets did not need to convince the people of what was to happen; they would see that for themselves soon enough. Their task was rather to prepare the people to receive and respond to the grace of the Lord, to help them see events with the eyes of faith, to be ready to live in his kingdom.

We see them, then, using every resource of poetry and imagery, of comparison and rhetoric, of challenge and dispute, rebuke and encouragement, that could flow from their inspired hearts. We cannot know how many responded or to what heights of vision they were raised. But we do know that down the centuries, and all the way into our own times, this poetic gospel has resounded with great power, and still can uplift the spirit and open the eyes of the heart as few words can.

> *Work, for I am with you!*
> *My Spirit is standing in your midst,*
> *fear not!* (Hag. 2.4–5).

Although Haggai is named after the *hag*, the great pilgrimage festival (his birth perhaps coinciding with the holy season), his prophesying has not that psalm-like, lyrical quality of Second Isaiah's and is furnished with pedantic detailing of the dates of his prophecies. Nevertheless, his themes are closely connected with those of the old autumn festivals. He is concerned to see the temple renewed and regards purified worship there as essential for the health and productivity of the land and the herds. He is also concerned with the role of the house of David, which he sees represented now by the governor Zerubbabel, the Lord's Servant and Chosen One, destined to be the great agent of divine authority, God's 'signet ring'.

Though his hopes for Zerubbabel could hardly be fulfilled, Haggai's words served at least to carry forward faith in the promises to David into the post-exilic era. On the issue of rebuilding the temple, Haggai's prophesying was more obviously fruitful, the re-dedication coming only six years after he began to stir up the people. The building was not so grand, and the octogenarians might see it as nothing. But Haggai gave further words of promise, and for over five centuries this 'second temple' was to stand at the heart of Jewish religion.

A very small book is Haggai's, and pedestrian in style. But here was a ministry of great value, both practical and imaginative. Scholars welcome the shaft of genuine historical light it sheds on a new epoch. To all it still urges that the building of the house of the Lord come first.

Truth has fallen in the city square (Isa. 59.14).

As with Second, so with Third Isaiah, no names of the prophets responsible have been preserved. Again we may conclude that this is because we are dealing with a group descended from Isaiah's circle, devoted to prolonging his witness, and not concerned to found new circles in the name of another prophetic master. In these chapters (56–66) continuity with Second Isaiah is evident, especially in chs. 60–62, except that most of the material now suits a context in Jerusalem soon after the end of enforced exile. It seems likely, then, that here we meet members of the Isaiah circle who were able to make the journey back to Zion. Even more than in the case of Haggai, we can feel the contrast between anticipatory hopes and the experienced reality. How reminiscent of the contrast between the hopes just before the disintegration of the Soviet empire and the difficult situations that have followed it!

At all events, the tensions and difficulties of that ancient time of 'liberation' have served to give a sharp edge to the new flow of prophecy from the Isaiah circle. Along with biting criticism of that society, there are radical words of enduring challenge, such as the comments on fasts, on access to the temple, and on the Lord's high freedom above all earthly places. Remarkable too are the long intercessions in the tradition of lamenting worship, with answering visions of hope. Though thick darkness cover the people, the glory of the Lord will rise sun-like upon his holy mountain. The gospel will be proclaimed to the oppressed, and a garland will replace the ashes of mourning. One prophecy even tells of God creating new heavens and earth, another of a unity of creatures in peace before the Lord – all peoples and animals, with no more hurting or destroying. So the vision of Isaiah is carried forward, the testimony maintained.

And the Lord whom you seek will suddenly come to his temple
(Mal. 3.1).

More than fifty years into the Persian period, with its partial liberation and its struggling restoration, comes a late messenger of the Lord, Malachi – if that really was his name. It is characteristic for those troubled times that his preserved sayings are formed around six occasions of dispute, moments of confrontation.

We found that he was especially familiar with the inner life of the temple and its priesthood. He attacks the irreverent service of the priests scathingly and reminds them of the priestly ideal – the mediator who would bring life and peace from God, serve with awe in the temple, teach and advise from a pure and faithful heart, turn back many from sin and guard the knowledge of God: in short, a person bound on the errands of God.

He spoke against ills in wider society, such as meanness to day-labourers and the cruel 'sending away' of wives. 'Have we not all one father, did not one God make us all?' – such was here his guiding thought. On many sides the prophet heard bitter objections to the faith. People saw little sign of a just God, and they said as much. And Malachi spoke with glowing imagery of the judgment that was near, the God whose advent would make justice triumph. It would be like a consuming fire, but the humble ones, who had lived in consciousness of God's being and will, would be remembered. They would know the rising of a sun of righteousness, a light of goodness, healing their wounds in the warmth of her rays.

> We have heard a revelation from the Lord,
> and among the nations (his) envoy has been sent
> (Obad. 1).

Obadiah, speaking for a prophetic circle, expresses a grave charge against the Edomites: arrogance and treachery. He sees their sin fostered by their sense of security in their fortress-cities, cleverly built in the mountain crags. Now that an envoy, an angelic spirit, has gone forth from the Lord's council to stir invaders against them, they must expect divine retribution. And there will be no defence in human cleverness.

So in Obadiah we met again the sense of divine purpose at work in the great international conflicts. Behind the forces that parade themselves as mighty is the God who alone has might, and who in his long-drawn purposes takes heed of pride and betrayal, humility and faithfulness: 'The Day of the Lord is near upon all nations! As you have done, it will be done to you.' Through the smoke and the din of human conflict, the prophet sees as near and surely coming the reign of the Lord, when saviours will ascend to mediate his rule from Mount Zion – a kingdom of salvation radiating from the house of David.

Before them the land is like the garden of Eden,
but after them a desolate wilderness! (Joel 2.3).

'Yahweh (alone) is God' – such is the testimony of Joel's name, which was common among the Levites who ministered in worship. Here was a prophet whose vision arose from signs, not among the nations, but in the natural world. The approach of the Day of the Lord he saw through the stripping of the land by locusts, and from the fires that ran through the bare fields. He sounded the call to penitence, to the wearing of sackcloth and the gathering in the courts of the temple to raise lamenting prayer to the Lord. Through the ravaging of the crops he discerned the approach of the exceeding great host of the Lord, at which heaven and earth were trembling.

From Joel's vivid poetry we gained a strong impression of the mood of the assembled people on such a penitential day, and the role of the prophets in bringing home to them the spiritual dimension in the physical catastrophes. We could see the exact place of the priestly choir, arrayed between temple entrance and the great altar in the open court. And we took part in that great turning of relief, when the prophet brought from the Lord an answer full of compassion and hope.

And then how awesome were the visions which subsequently unfolded – the Spirit poured out upon all kinds of people, enriching them with prophecies, dreams and visions; the peoples gathered in their multitudes in the valley of decision, the valley of judgment; the sun turned to darkness, and the moon to blood; and at the last, the fountain of life that flowed from the house of the Lord, while mountains ran with wine and milk, and valleys rippled with water!

In Joel's time, insects were not just insects, but servants of God. Likewise bushfires. Through them came the challenge to deeper levels of existence, that began with repentance and prayer, the rending of hearts and the return to the Lord, and the hope of finding his compassion in the day when this world collapses.

Speak truth to one another;
  judge in your gates with truth and for the cause of peace;
do not plan in your hearts harm for your neighbour;
  and do not love false oaths (Zech. 8.16–17).

In Zechariah we met one of the prophets who illustrate the ministry needed when a more favourable era is coming, bringing its own kind of problems. He may have been given his name ('Yahweh has remembered') because at his birth among the exiles the dawn of the new era was already discerned. In the re-emerging Jerusalem he was a figure of encouragement. The mountains of debris were heavy upon the soul of the royal governor. Zechariah assured him that the mountains left by the old tragedy would be cleared – not by human might, but by the Lord's Spirit. The temple would be built and blessed, the priests would again serve the Lord there. The streets would again be happy places, where people could grow old and enjoy the sight of little children at play in the streets. But again and again Zechariah wove through his promises the call to humble faith, truth and compassion.

The strength and richness of his ministry flowed from an extraordinary inner life – his visions in the night, his openness to heavenly instruction. From a visionary world of heavenly horses and riders, bronze mountains at the entrance of heaven, angel-blacksmiths that beat down the horns of earth's military powers, flying objects in the form of a giant scroll and a barrel borne by witches – from such visions and their inspired interpretations, Zechariah came to rulers and people with words that made all the harsh circumstances glow with the good meaning of God.

I took the thirty pieces of silver
and threw them into the treasury
in the house of the Lord (Zech. 11.13).

In Zechariah's time, just as in Isaiah's, it was still possible to think of the group sitting at the feet of a sacred leader as a 'sign' (Zech. 3.7; Isa. 8.18). One may wonder if Zechariah himself had similar associates, conscious of a common vocation, and whether from them comes the further body of oracles in Zech. 9–14. We noted that here the person and the circumstances of Zechariah are no longer evident, yet no new name of authorship is given. In the varied contents, old elements may mingle with some of Hebrew prophecy's latest words. Indeed, an abolition of prophets is foretold, for they are inspired, it is suggested, by an unclean spirit (Zech. 13.2).

These chapters, without clear background and often enigmatic, yet strike deep notes. One example makes us think of the Suffering Servant: 'I will pour out on the house of David and the inhabitants of Jerusalem the Spirit of grace and supplication, and when they look on him whom they have pierced, they shall mourn for him as one mourns for an only child (12.10) . . . Awake O sword against my shepherd, against the man who stands beside me (13.7)!'

Near the beginning of the collection is an echo of a hymn from the royal rites which taught the righteousness and humility required of the king (9.9–10). Towards the end, the autumn festival, which had been so important for the national religion and so also for nation-wide prophecy, is presented as 'the feast of Booths' where the kingship of the Lord is celebrated, the winter rains granted, and the participation of all nations desired (14.16–18).

Links with the New Testament are quite frequent, and the very last words give an example: 'And in that day there shall no longer be a trader in the house of the Lord' (14.21).

You are concerned for the plant which cost you no trouble . . . and should I not have pity on Nineveh, this huge city with more than a hundred and twenty thousand not knowing their right from their left, and also many animals?
(Jonah 4.10–11).

In its way the book of Jonah is another indication of the end of prophecy of the kind we have been studying. For here the one who is burning with a God-given conviction does not himself come forward with a 'Thus says the Lord'. Instead he tells an engaging tale of several episodes and many marvels. True, he weaves his story around a prophet of old; but the message emerges as a contrast to this prophet's atttitude.

The ending of the story – not with a resolution, but with a question – shows how the tale is aimed to convert the hearers. It is for them to answer, freeing themselves of spiritual meanness, and aligning themselves with the compassionate heart of God. Such telling of a story is not prophecy as such; but ancient prophets could resort to it (II Samuel 12), and now, after the demise of great prophecy, it was to become more and more the way to open eyes and hearts to the promptings of God.

Go on your way, Daniel, for these words are to remain secret and sealed till the time of the end (Dan. 12.9).

We found that in the Hebrew Bible the Book of Daniel was not placed among the prophetic books, but among the miscellaneous 'Writings'. Nevertheless, it was helpful for us to include it in our study, in order to appreciate the difference between the apocalyptic literature and the older prophecy. We saw that the Book of Daniel was an early example of a kind of writing that flourished from the mid-second century BCE into the first century CE. Such writings reveal mysteries in a time of crisis. From visions presented as if given to ancient patriarchs and kept secret until the present time, the message comes that the current tyranny will assuredly give way to the reign of God and his saints.

In forming their writings in this mould, the authors effectively convey the sense that the persecutors have no power to determine their own continuance. In God's long-formed purpose their time has been allotted; the coming of the good kingdom is certain and fixed. And just as certain it is that those who now suffer for God's sake will then have their reward.

Such writings belonged to a time when the harsh powers of the state were directed to liquidating a particular faith-group. The stories in the Book of Daniel join the strange visions and interpretations in strengthening the persecuted for the hour of trial. The context was thus different from that of our prophets, and indeed centuries lie between them. The prophet bringing critical oracles to the assembled nation had long disappeared. The scriptures too had passed through a long history and their limits were almost fixed. Of all the Jewish apocalypses, only Daniel was able to edge into the officially recognized scripture.

In its message about the kingdom of God, the one like a son of man, and the rising of the dead, the Book of Daniel offers much of importance, and forms a bridge from the older scriptures to the thought-world of the New Testament.

Bibliography

of works cited and suggested reading

Anderson, B.W., *The Living World of the Old Testament*, Longman, 4th edn 1988

St Augustine, *The Confessions*, translated by E.B. Pusey in 1838, reissued in Everyman's Library by Dent, London and Dutton, New York, no date

Baly, Denis, *Basic Biblical Geography*, Fortress Press, Philadelphia 1987

Blenkinsopp, Joseph, *A History of Prophecy in Israel*, Westminster John Knox, Louisville KY, revised 1996

Chadwick, N. Kershaw, *Poetry and Prophecy*, CUP 1942

Chitty, Derwas J., *The Desert A City: An Introduction to the Study of Egyptian and Palestinian Monasteries under the Christian Empire*, Mowbray, 2nd edn 1977

Davies, G.I., *Ancient Hebrew Inscriptions*, CUP 1992

Eaton, John, *Festal Drama in Deutero-Isaiah*, SPCK 1979

Eaton, John, *The Psalms Come Alive*, Mowbray 1984

Eaton, John, *Interpreted By Love. Expositions of Great Old Testament Passages*, Bible Reading Fellowship 1994

Emmerson, Grace I., *Isaiah 56–66, Old Testament Guides* series, JSOT Press 1992

Engnell, Ivan, *The Messiah in the Old Testament*, SCM Press 1956

Engnell, Ivan, *Critical Essays on the Old Testament*, SPCK 1970

Frank, H.T., *An Archaeological Companion to the Bible*, Abingdon Press, Nashville and SCM Press 1972

Gibson, John, *Canaanite Myths and Legends*, T.& T. Clark 1978

Gordon, Robert P., 'From Mari to Moses: Prophecy at Mari and in Ancient Israel' in *Of Prophets' Visions and the Wisdom of Sages* ed H.A. McKay and D.J.A. Clines, JSOT Press 1993, pp.63–79

Grabbe, Lester L., 'Prophets, Priests, Diviners and Sages in Ancient Israel' in McKay and Clines (eds), *Of Prophets' Visions . . .*(see under Gordon), pp.43–62

Hastings, James, *Dictionary of the Bible*, 1909, revised by F.C.Grant and H.H.Rowley, T.& T. Clark 1963

Hooker, Morna D., *The Signs of a Prophet: The Prophetic Actions of Jesus*, SCM Press and TPI, Valley Forge 1997

Johnson, A.R., 'The Prophet in Israelite Worship' in *The Expository Times*, vol. xlvii , 1935–36, pp.312–19

King, Philip J., *Jeremiah: An Archaeological Companion*, Westminster John Knox, Louisville KY 1993

May, H.G., *The Oxford Bible Atlas*, 3rd edn revised by John Day, OUP 1984

North, C.R., *The Suffering Servant in Deutero-Isaiah*, OUP, 2nd edn 1956

Martin Palmer, Man-Ho Kwok, Jay Ramay (translators), *Tao Te Ching. The New Translation*, Element Classic Editions, Element 1994

E.G. Parrinder, *African Traditional Religion*, Sheldon Press, 3rd edn 1974

Prévost, Jean-Pierre, *How to Read the Prophets*, SCM Press and Continuum, New York 1996

Pritchard, J.B. (ed), *Ancient Near Eastern Texts*, Princeton University Press, 2nd edn 1955

Ringgren, Helmer, *The Messiah in the Old Testament*, SCM Press 1956

Ringgren, Helmer, 'Prophecy in the Ancient Near East' in *Israel's Prophetic Tradition*, ed R. Coggins et al., CUP 1982, pp.1–11

Skinner, J., *Prophecy and Religion. Studies in the Life of Jeremiah*, CUP 1922

Stacey, W. David, *Prophetic Drama in the Old Testament*, Epworth Press 1990

Waley, Arthur, *The Way and Its Power: A Study of the Tao Te Ching*, Allen and Unwin 1934

Wright, G.E., *Biblical Archaeology*, Westminster Press, Philadelphia and Duckworth 1957

Yutang, Lin (ed), *The Wisdom of China*, (includes translation and comment on the Tao Te Ching) Michael Joseph 1944

Index of Subjects

Also see Contents page

Index of Biblical References

Also see Contents page. Individual references within the books under discussion are not indexed

Matthew		11.1–10	164	Hebrews	
1.23	75			1.1	176
Mark		Galatians		Revelation	
1.6	77	1.11–14	10	4;5;21;22	125